Soft-Spoken
Parenting

Soft-Spoken
Parenting

50 Ways to Not Lose Your Temper With Your Kids

H. WALLACE GODDARD, PH.D.

SILVERLEAF
PRESS

Silverleaf Press Books are available exclusively
through Independent Publishers Group.

For details, write or telephone
Independent Publishers Group, 814 North Franklin St.
Chicago, IL 60610, (312) 337-0747

Silverleaf Press
8160 South Highland Dr.
Sandy, UT 84093

ISBN-13: 978-1-933317-88-5

Printed in the United States of America

The universe is full of magical things patiently waiting for our wits to grow sharper.

Eden Phillpots

Contents

Acknowledgements

Thanks to the most patient and kind person I have ever known, my dear wife, Nancy. Thanks also to our children, their spouses, and their children for their patience with me as I learn to practice what I preach. Thanks to my wonderful parents and ancestors who planted a love of life deep in my soul. Thanks to those—scholars and friends alike—who have taught me about this important subject. Thanks to you, kind reader, for your efforts to bring more kindness and goodness to the world we all share.

Introduction

We all get angry. Sometimes it is nothing more than simmering irritation. Other times it is fire in our soul. Our ears burn and every cell tenses.

Yet even as we ready for the holy battle, we have the sneaking suspicion that our anger is not good for us or for our unlucky target.

We are right. Anger is very destructive.

So this book is for normal parents—parents like me and you—who love their children but get angry too readily. This book is for parents like us who have gotten so upset about some minor offense that we have launched into an endless lecture quite heedless of the devastation we were heaping on our children. This is for parents who find themselves simmering with the combination of stress in their own lives and misdemeanors in their children's lives.

This book is for parents like us who want their children to become good, caring, loving adults and wish that we were better parents so we didn't get in their way.

You're Not Alone

Haim Ginott, the parenting genius and author of several books, described our dilemma in the introduction to his classic *Between Parent and Child*: "No parent wakes up in the morning planning to make a child's life miserable. No mother or father says, 'Today, I'll yell, nag, and humiliate my child whenever possible.' On the contrary, in the morning many parents resolve, 'This is going to be a peaceful day. No yelling, no arguing, and no fighting.' Yet, in spite of good intentions, the unwanted war breaks out again. Once more we find ourselves saying things we do not mean, in a tone we do not like."[1]

In fact, those of us who are most vulnerable to anger may be those who have stronger emotions of all kinds. We love more passionately, we live more joyously. That is a blessing. But there is a downside to every good thing. Along with the gift of fire (enthusiasm, passion, gusto, zeal), we have the challenge of channeling, managing, and training our fire.

Fire can warm and cook. It can also scorch and destroy. Let's begin by trying to better understand anger.

The Pleasure of Anger

There is something wonderfully satisfying about anger. Frederick Buechner said it elegantly: "Of the seven deadly sins, anger is possibly the most fun. To lick your wounds, to smack your lips over grievances long past, to roll over your tongue the prospect of bitter confrontations still to come, to savor to the last toothsome morsel both the pain you are given and the pain you are giving back—in many ways it is a feast fit for a king."[2]

The excesses of anger are captured in a story I read about a woman who returned damaged merchandise to a store. She launched into the customer service rep with a vengeance. He listened patiently. Finally, after several minutes of listening patiently, he interrupted her and asked, "Ma'am, suppose we refund your money, provide you another one without charge, close the store, and shoot the manager. Would that be satisfactory?"

Anger tends to take us over. It is much like throwing a match into dry tinder. It starts readily, grows quickly, and is hard to stop. Before we know it, fire can destroy everything in sight.

The Assumptions behind Anger

Even as we violate our conscience by insulting those we love, it is quite possible for us to feel virtuous. We may think, "You are wrong or bad and I am helping you by straightening you out." Consider some of the common assumptions behind most anger.

1. Anger is real. Anger tends to feel wonderfully authentic. "This is truth. I hadn't seen it before. But now I do!" We discover that our child has stolen from a neighbor, hurt a sibling, or told a lie. We feel that flash of indignation. Suddenly it all makes sense. The child needs rebuke!

2. "I must be honest with you." When we discover something awful, it seems as if we must deal with it immediately. It would be irresponsible to neglect our moral duty. We need to talk about it. The "truth" explodes from us. We can't seem to keep it in.

3. "I must deal with anger by getting it out." "With all this feeling inside me, if I don't get it out, I'll explode." So I tell my child just what she has done wrong—in angry, indignant tones.

4. "After getting my anger out, I will feel better." Most of us assume that the expression of anger is cathartic. "After I have fully expressed my indignation, I will feel relieved and peaceful."

5. "After I've told you what's wrong with you, you can do better." It seems that our child has been blind to some truth that we have discovered. When we point out his error, he or she should be able to make better choices in the future.

Anger seemingly has all the satisfactions of a crusade: a worthy cause, plenty of emotion, an opportunity to make the world a better place, and a deep feeling of satisfaction.

Unfortunately for those of us who get angry readily, all of the five ideas above are almost entirely false. The crusade turns out to be a slaughter of innocents. The truths about anger are very different from the common beliefs.

The Truth about Anger

Years of research have helped us better understand anger. It is generally not the positive, beneficial force that many have believed it to be. The following propositions about anger are generally closer to the truth than those listed above.

1. Anger is a liar. Our thoughts when we are angry are not calm, sensible, or balanced. They are narrow—we focus on one small part of the story or one small part of the child's character. Anger is almost always irrational and unbalanced. "Rare is the person who can weigh the faults of others without putting his thumb on the scales," wrote Byron J. Langenfield.[3] We get taken hostage by an unhelpful emotion and our reason and civility break down. Instead of seeking understanding, we begin to seek a conviction of the person.

2. Angry times are bad times for honesty. Anger tends to focus on the negative. But the negative part is not the whole story. It is not even the most important part of the story. Honesty may not be as important as integrity, which acknowledges a larger reality than the complaint. When we are angry is not the best time to say everything we are thinking.

3. There are ways to deal with anger besides pouring molten lava on those we love. The popular belief that if we do not express our anger, it will

explode—or come out in sick forms—is simply mistaken. When we dwell on our anger it grows. When we set it aside, it can cool. Anger is a little like tasting very hot soup. We must allow it to cool a little before we eat it or we will burn our mouths.

4. We often feel quite conflicted after we have blown up with people we love. After unloading on a child, our minds may be insisting that we were right and that they needed to hear it. But our hearts tell us that we have violated the contract of love that binds us together. We have turned against those we swore to bless and protect, to encourage and to teach. Our conscience, if we listen to it, aches when we unleash wrath on our children.

5. When we get angry at our children, it often leaves them unmotivated, even despairing. Think about times when you were the receiver rather than the deliverer of wrath. Were you energized and motivated by the tirade? Most likely you were hurt and your first thought was counter-anger or revenge. It is possible that you acquiesced, but you were probably not motivated or energized. The same is true with our children. When we unload on them, they don't usually feel encouraged. They probably feel burdened, hopeless, and resentful.

As a wise man has said, being angry is like drinking poison and waiting for your enemy to die. Anger destroys us. It also damages our most cherished relationships. It gives control of our lives to irrational and unhelpful passion.

Society may excuse—even encourage and model—smart-alecky, diminishing, and sarcastic attacks on people. Hollywood regularly recommends such an approach. I cannot count the number of movies in which an unmotivated group of children got a vigorous scolding from an indignant adult and the children promptly reformed themselves. Of course the children won some championship. If we believe the media, we believe that scolding is good motivation. Research on parenting says otherwise. As Sigsgaard observed:

> Scolding and punishment frighten children. Their natural tendency when scared is to cling to their mother, but she is the one doing the scolding, and in doing so she is pushing the child away from her. This causes additional anxiety, and the child is frustrated—unable to act on his or her natural impulses. The people who are supposed to shield the child from anxiety and comfort the child are instead the source of an anxiety from which the child can find no shelter. This means that repeated and/or severe scolding may damage the child's fundamental trust.[5]

A Better Approach

The two central themes in effective childrearing are consistent nurture and positive guidance. To nurture a child suggests that we protect, support, and encourage that child. Nurture involves giving time, interest, and affection. There are great challenges in doing this well. Effective nurture requires us to shut down the noise in our own heads long enough to really see and understand the child and his or her world. This is one of the hardest things adults ever do! We tend to want children to effortlessly slipstream into our world and doings. They don't. Nothing will upend our tidy lives as much as having children. (And, in my view, nothing will generate the meaning and growth in adults that nurturing children will!)

The second ingredient of effective parenting is positive guidance. Children need wise and patient adults who will show them and teach them how to be responsible, resilient, and loving human beings. Yikes! This requires remarkable knowledge and character.

And I believe that Nature has so constructed us that our normal, automatic responses are almost always counterproductive. This principle is akin to the conspiracy of nature that physicists talk about. And it may seem very annoying. Yet most of us would never have it otherwise.

Thomas Paine wrote familiar words about the value of freedom. Consider how these same sentiments apply to parenting. "The harder the conflict, the more glorious the triumph. What we obtain too cheap, we esteem too lightly: it is dearness only that gives every thing its value. Heaven knows how to put a proper price upon its goods; and it would be strange indeed if so celestial an article as [healthy, happy children] should not be highly rated."[6]

Indeed. We must be willing to pay a price if we want children who grow into strong and caring adults. The currency of the childrearing realm is character. While we cannot change our characters or our children's characters overnight, we can make patient, earnest personal growth the focus of our efforts.

So the 50 strategies described in this book entail real effort. We often must change the way we think. Sometimes we must manage how we feel. Often we must change how we act. And, in the end, we become better people because we invested in human capital.

Getting Free of Contention

Anger often seems irresistible. A child breaks a glass or hits a sibling and we erupt. Can such an automatic process be interrupted? Can volcanic anger be replaced with civil helpfulness? It seems that it would be easier to turn the mighty Mississippi upstream than to redirect the energy of wrath. We feel helpless in the face of our passion.

The problem of anger doesn't actually begin with the misbehavior that seems to cause it. It begins much sooner. Often we remain quite unaware of the background of irritation in our moods that sets the stage for anger. Sometimes our children get the residue of disappointment from work or loneliness in our souls.

There is another problem with anger. We may be quite unaware of the assumptions that we impose on those around us. We each have a script filled with notions about how people should act. When someone acts differently, we may become quite indignant.

When we act as if everyone should follow our rules, we set ourselves up for chronic frustration. There is a devious kind of pride in imposing our assumptions on everyone around us. In contrast, humility is a wonderful openness. We are more free to appreciate the diverse ways that people— including our children—think and act.

For example, a mother awoke on her birthday smelling the aromas of a delightful breakfast. She rested in bed anticipating a birthday surprise. After a long wait, one of the children came into her room, "As a birthday surprise, we cooked our own breakfast."

The mother could be quite angry that the children did not bring her any breakfast. Or she can be grateful for the children's growing thoughtfulness and self-sufficiency. Of course she might also tell them that she loves to have breakfast with them and would be glad to be included next time.

You can see the vital role of humility. When we are humble—when we don't insist on having the world operate by our rules—we are less likely to be irritated by differences. We are less likely to impose our meanings on someone else's behavior. The anger problem has deep roots—way down into our assumptions.

At the heart of much of our anger is a painfully human reaction. A child spills a glass of milk and, somewhere in our souls, we react: "How could you do this to me?" Of course we have been trained to use other words: "You need to be more careful," or "How could you be so clumsy?" But behind the words there may be a more self-oriented reaction: "Why should your clumsiness make me late for work or mess up my table or…" In other words, "How could you do this to me?" Anger is a self-centered reaction to inconvenience or disappointment.

We can choose to respond to spilt milk in gracious ways: "Oops. The milk spilled. I'll grab you a towel," or "Too bad. We all spill sometimes," or "Cool! I have wanted to do milk painting on the table for a long time. What shall we draw?"

When we act with the child's needs in mind, we act very differently. When we understand that our children are doing the best they know how in a big, confusing world in which they often feel awkward and powerless, we can act compassionately. When a child falls short because of lack of wisdom or experience, we can teach rather than punish.

More than we realize, our anger hurts and frightens our children. We do not teach our children to avoid fighting and quarrelling by fighting and quarrelling with them.

Anger is addictive. A couple of marriage scholars have described the satisfaction of having someone to blame:

> How wonderful to have someone to blame! How wonderful to live with one's nemesis! You may be miserable, but you feel forever in the right. You may be fragmented, but you feel absolved of all the blame for it.[7]

Let's return to Buechner's observation. At the beginning of this section we quoted him describing anger as a feast fit for a king. He finishes his observation with the following words: "The chief drawback is that what you are wolfing down is yourself. The skeleton at the feast is you."[8]

Anger can destroy us and our families. There are better ways. We can use soft-spoken parenting—parenting that is filled with both compassion and wisdom.

The Science of Anger

Research has shown that hostility can damage our hearts. Those who are angry are five times as likely to have serious heart problems as those who aren't. Anger is bad for the heart! In fact, "hostility [is] a strong predictor of mortality rate—death from all causes combined."[9] If you want to ruin your health, be angry.

There are three parts to the anger that destroys us: cynical mistrust of others, frequent angry feelings, and aggressive behavior. For example, if a person is following you too closely when you are driving your car, you may at first wonder if they are stupid, then you may feel angry, then perhaps you will act to spite them by deliberately slowing down. All the while, you are damaging your own heart.

The same thing happens in our relationships with our children. We may find that they have not washed the dishes or done their homework. We may find that they have picked on a younger brother or sister.

Our first reaction is cynicism: "That is a lazy kid," "I knew I couldn't trust him," "That kid never thinks of anyone but himself!"

And we get angry. We feel indignant. We want to punish the child. (Any time we are inclined to hurt someone, we should question the impulse.)

Then we get aggressive. The aggression may be verbal or physical. We may lecture or yell at children. We may spank them, shove them, or drag them to their rooms.

All of this is bad for our heart. And it is bad for our relationships. As therapist Bernie Zilbergeld said about anger in marriage: "I cannot count the number of times that married couples tell me: 'I've got all this anger bottled up and I need to get it out.' Sure you do, and I'll be happy to cater the divorce."[10]

As Carol Tavris has observed in her classic book on anger, "Most of the time, expressing anger makes people angrier, solidifies an angry attitude, and establishes a hostile habit. If you keep quiet about momentary irritations and distract yourself with pleasant activity until your fury simmers down, chances are you will feel better, and feel better faster, than if you let yourself go in a shouting match."[11]

Anger has a way of focusing—even narrowing—our attention. This may be very useful if we are preparing to fight off attacking wolves or marauding bandits. In those situations, the focus can be very helpful. It allows us to put all our resources and extraordinary energy into the service of defending ourselves.

That same focus is entirely unhelpful if you are dealing with family members who spilled the milk or came home late. In those cases, the focus may over-energize an aggressive attack. Rather than think of the misdeeds as assaults on us or civilized living, it is more helpful to think of the misdeeds in the context of the children's histories, intentions, and circumstances.

Returning again to Tavris: "Because anger is fomented, maintained, and inflamed by the statements we make to ourselves and others when we are provoked ('What a thoughtless lout!' 'Who does she think she is!'), [we can learn] to control anger the same way, by reinterpreting the supposed provocation: 'Maybe he's having a rough day'; 'She must be very unhappy if she would do such a thing.' This is what people who are slow to anger do naturally: They empathize with the other person's behavior and try to find justifications for it."[12]

When we are tempted to be angry with a child, we can apply compassion. We can try to see the world through their less-experienced eyes. We can try to understand their life, challenges, and personality. In fact, there are many things we can do to turn away wrath.

Emotion Coaching

There is an area of research on parenting that is particularly relevant to soft-spoken parenting. It deals with the ways parents react to their children's strong feelings. John Gottman, who may be the world's leading scholar on couple relationships, has also studied parent-child relationships.

Gottman encourages parents to be aware of their children's emotions. Rather than seeing their strong emotions as dangerous, we can see them as an opportunity for closeness and for teaching. When children are upset, we can offer emotional support: "This is a big disappointment to you." "You feel hurt and angry." Such simple statements help the child know that we notice, care about, and can relate to the things they feel. It can also help children understand what they are feeling as we help them process their feelings.

For many parents the big surprise in this process is that we can—and should—show understanding for our children's feelings without necessarily agreeing with their feelings or endorsing their impulses. In fact we can show great compassion while also setting limits on behavior. "You're really angry with your brother! You would like to beat him up for the mess he made. I know you're frustrated."

As the child feels more peaceful, we can move to the next step: "Let's figure out a way to talk with your brother about this." There is a clear understanding that we never hurt or attack other people. We do not accept fighting and quarreling. But we can coach our children through emotional upheavals toward peacefulness and, ultimately, positive action.

Consider the familiar childhood complaint, "I hate my brother!" Parents quite naturally push back. "You don't hate your brother! You love him."

Hmmm. I figure that the only people who never hated their brothers never had any.

It is not helpful to deny the child's anger. We can show our understanding with well-chosen words: "Right now you're so mad you'd like to punch him in the nose." "I can see why you're upset. If I had spent that much time building a castle only to have it knocked over, I would be angry too!"

We keep showing understanding until the child feels more peaceful. This may require many rounds of compassionate statements. It may also involve sitting together in a rocking chair or taking a walk or letting a child cry it out.

When the child feels peaceful, then we launch a problem-solving process: "What do you think we can do to prevent this problem with your brother?" Torture and incarceration are not options. But we can help the child think of sensible precautions. "Would it help to build your castle on your desk so that your brother can't reach it? Would it help to keep your door closed when you are working on a project? Could you teach your brother how to help you rather than destroy your work?"

The more a child feels peaceful the more likely he or she is to find a good solution.

Consider another great example from Haim Ginott. Carol, age twelve, was tense and tearful. Her favorite cousin was going home after staying with her during the summer.

> Carol (with tears in her eyes): Susie is going away. I'll be all alone again.

Mom: You'll find another friend.

Carol: I'll be so lonely.

Mom: You'll get over it.

Carol: Oh, mother! (Sobs.)

Mom: You are twelve years old and still such a crybaby!

Carol gave mother a deadly look and escaped to her room, closing the door behind her.

This episode should have had a happier ending. A child's feeling must be taken seriously, even when the situation itself is not very serious. In Mom's eyes a separation may be too minor a crisis for tears, but her response need not have lacked sympathy. Mother might have said to herself, "Carol is distressed. I can help her best by showing that I understand what pains her." To her daughter she might have said any or all of the following:

"It will be lonely without Susie."
"You miss her already."
"It's hard to be apart when you're used to being together."
"The house must seem kind of empty to you without
Susie around."

Such compassionate responses are at the heart of soft-spoken parenting.

Soft-Spoken Parenting

Anger—and the resulting irrationality—may be a small problem or a large problem in your family. Whatever the amount, let's imagine your family using better ways of preventing, managing, and overcoming conflict. Let's previsualize peaceful possibilities.

First let's imagine that you have strengthened relationships so that most of the time family members enjoy each other. Little complaints don't become big battles. Family members laugh, work, and play together feeling safe, loving, and affectionate. Imagine that family members feel this way most of the time. That is prevention!

Second, let's imagine that you have good ways of dealing with those power-surges of anger that catch you unawares. Maybe you've learned ways of thinking differently about the irritations in family life. Maybe you've learned ways to delay or respond positively to feelings of anger. But, instead of getting dragged to foolishness by strong feelings, you have learned to take charge of them. You have learned how to make peace and consideration the themes of your parenting.

Third, let's imagine that you have learned good ways of slowing down anger that has gotten started or making repairs when your temper has gotten the best of you. Picture your family without the pains of extended resentful silences. Picture your family quickly pushing anger and evil out the back door and throwing open the windows to light, warmth, and love.

Anger should be as rare a visitor to our homes as is the appliance repairman. Anger does happen, but peace, cooperation, and appreciation can be the central features of our family life.

Imagining a better family life does not make it better automatically. But it provides vision and purpose for our efforts. And it is far better than ruminating over a long history of family brush fires.

So imagine your family as a lovely garden filled with brilliant blooms, gentle breezes, warm sunshine, singing birds, and peaceful repose. There may be an occasional mosquito seeking a victim, but you rejoice in the blessing of loving relationships.

May it be so for you and for all of us.

Process of Change

As you study the 50 strategies for keeping a hold on your temper, remember that some things we can do will help us change for the better. However, some things—even done with the best of intentions—will actually make things worse.

For example, inventorying mistakes and failures may evoke negative feelings and reactions. Carrying around a burden of guilt does not help us travel better. Recognizing our mistakes, however, will help us if it simply causes us to be open to new and better ways. Beyond that, it is a burden that hinders our progress.

It can actually be very energizing to celebrate our victories. We review those times—few or many—that we have caught ourselves sliding down the slope toward an angry attack and have taken a mental time-out to soothe ourselves. We cherish those times. We think about the things we did to interrupt our anger. We turn our successes into both optimism and wisdom. We focus on soft-spoken parenting.

There is another key to change. Each of us has different natural gifts. Some of the strategies described in this book will fit you wonderfully well. Others will not. It is important for us, as parents, to put our energy into those that fit us. For example, the energetic enthusiastic parent will probably never learn to become perfectly tranquil. But she might learn to become good at apologizing.

As you find strategies in this book that fit you and inspire ideas for new responses, you might profitably pre-experience your responses in situations where that strategy would be useful. We can think through a typical blow-up and plan what we will say and how we will act the next time this blow-up occurs. We might even plan what we will do with the unhelpful feelings that inevitably arise. It might be helpful to write out the plan or to pre-imagine it several times so that we are ready when the crisis arises. The following chart will help you evaluate each strategy's value to you.

Finally, we should learn from mistakes. We all make them! We all act foolishly at times. Yet the victory of a peaceful family will go to those who are determined to keep bringing healing goodness and wisdom to their family life. We should be as patient with our own learning process as an ideal parent would be.

When I am asked to define the effective parent, I think of the story of a middle-aged man who decided to take better care of himself. He made a resolve to eat better and exercise more. One day when he showed up at work with a very rich coffee cake, his co-workers chided him: "We thought you turned over a new leaf." He smiled angelically: "Just a minute. This is a very special coffeecake. Normally I wouldn't eat something like this. But this morning I found myself in front of the bakery and saw this coffee cake. It looked very special to me. So I prayed, 'Father, if you want me to have that coffee cake, make a parking place for me right in front of the bakery.' And, sure enough, on the eighth time around the block, there was the parking place."

Great parenting is done by those who are willing to keep going around the block—those who are willing to try new things and never give up.

The Strategies

1.

Get Your Heart Right

Have you ever felt so serene and peaceful that you loved the whole world?

I remember as a young father coming home from work after a busy day. There were many household tasks that clamored for my attention. But Andy was building a tree house. He wanted help from his dad. I chose to set aside other demands and join him. We had a great time together—partners in a noble undertaking.

We constantly make choices. Usually they are made so automatically that we are not even aware of the process. We are hostages to our moods. We come home from work tired and distracted and we ignore our children. We go about our duties in a fog.

But it doesn't have to be that way. We can choose to tune in. As we stop to pick up a child or approach the house, we can pull up our mental menu. We can look over the options:

> Grumpy and unavailable
> Pleasant but mildly distracted
> Cordial but not really connected
> Tuned in

We can choose. And the choice makes a difference. If all of us chose to be lovingly engaged every day, anger would not be a problem.

But we are not and it is. Most of the time we operate between mild irritation and total annoyance. That is part of living in a demanding world where hassles and demands assail us constantly.

So the blessed state of serenity does not come to us automatically. We can make choices. Sometimes serenity and loving involvement will seem beyond reach. In fact, there will be times when we say to a child, "I really want to build a Lego castle with you. Unfortunately, I must do a couple of things first. Can we build after dinner?"

There will be other times when dint of will is not enough to chase away a nagging irritability. We may need to take a few minutes to breathe deeply and reflect on good times. Or you may need to send yourself to your room as I have done. "Family, right now I am an ornery, tired sack of bones. Because I just might blow up, I am sending myself to my room for 10 minutes to calm down. Let's pray that the parent that emerges from the room is a better one than you have now."

Over the course of time our children will see us distracted, irritable, engaged, and fun. Our efforts to choose serenity and compassion make it more likely that our children will grow up feeling loved, and valued.

．

So any process that keeps our hearts tender, compassionate, and patient should be cherished. Maybe the process that works for you is meditation, prayer, journaling, conscious gratitude, savoring nature, or remembering great times with family members. If we choose to get our hearts right, we become soft-spoken parents.

Reflection

Think of a time when you have had your heart right. How did it feel? What helped you get there? How can you get there again? How can you make that experience more common for you?

Applying this Strategy

☐ I don't think this will work for me.

☐ This is something I am already good at and use regularly to good effect.

☐ This is something I haven't tried but would like to try.

> Next time [insert your parenting dilemma] happens, I'm going to try [insert your personal solution that applies this strategy].
>
> > Write a plan.
> >
> > Visualize yourself doing it.

☐ This is something I have tried but need to practice.

> Next time [insert your parenting dilemma] happens, I'm going to try [insert your personal solution that applies this strategy].
>
> > Write a plan.
> >
> > Visualize yourself doing it.

Notes on progress: _____

_____

_____

_____

_____

2.

Just Say "No" to Anger

Anger makes a lot of bold claims that it can't support. It claims to represent some reality when in fact it represents a contorted misunderstanding. The misunderstanding that undergirds anger is the belief "my way is the right way" and when you deviate from it, you're messed up. And there's actually another misunderstanding in anger: It is that chewing people out causes them to behave better.

The prominent psychologist Jonathan Haidt summarized a whole body of research when he described a troublesome human foible:

"We all commit selfish and shortsighted acts, but our inner [defense] lawyer ensures that we do not blame ourselves or our allies for them. We are thus convinced of our own virtue, but quick to see bias, greed, and duplicity in others. We are often correct about others' motives, but as any conflict escalates we begin to exaggerate grossly, we weave a story in which pure virtue (our side) is in battle with pure vice (theirs)."[13]

When we know that anger aims to make fools of us all, we may decide to just say "no" to anger. Now, for those of us who have practiced anger for years, this is not a single, one-time decision. We will decide again and again.

Maybe anger is like that pair of plaid pants each of us bought somewhere in our youth. We were enchanted with them when we bought them. But over time we sensed that we were making fools of ourselves. We stopped wearing them.

We can do something like that with anger. Knowing that it keeps us from seeing truly and acting helpfully, we resist it. We seek to calm ourselves. We try to turn indignation into amusement—we laugh at the human condition. We ask forgiveness of those we have insulted. We seek better ways to find common cause.

I taught high school for some years after I graduated from college. Our school principal asked all faculty and staff to help enforce rules of civility. For example, he asked that we encourage people to remove their hats when they were inside the school building.

One day as people were streaming into the building for an evening basketball game, I noted a giant fellow who was wearing a hat. It is important to note that he had the stature of Goliath. Dutifully I approached him and asked if he would mind taking off his hat. He turned to me and asked if I would like him to knock my head off. To me it seemed like a bad trade-off. I dropped the hat issue. It wasn't hard.

Sometimes we feel that anger will not be denied. It must be expressed. My experience is that we are quite able to control our demands when it assures our survival. So the most common victims for our anger may be those who are unlikely to knock our heads off.

To prevent spilling anger on our relatively powerless children, we can imagine them as Goliaths. Or we can remind ourselves that these are the most important people in our lives. Or we can simply decide to say "no" to anger.

Reflection

Think of a time when you just said "no" to anger. How did it feel? What helped you get there? How can you get there again? How can you make that experience more common for you?

Applying this Strategy

☐ I don't think this will work for me.

☐ This is something I am already good at and use regularly to good effect.

☐ This is something I haven't tried but would like to try.

　　Next time [insert your parenting dilemma] happens, I'm going to try [insert your personal solution that applies this strategy].

　　　　Write a plan.

　　　　Visualize yourself doing it.

☐ This is something I have tried but need to practice.

　　Next time [insert your parenting dilemma] happens, I'm going to try [insert your personal solution that applies this strategy].

　　　　Write a plan.

　　　　Visualize yourself doing it.

Notes on progress: _____

_____

_____

_____

_____

3.

Choose Laughter over Accusation

Some years ago when our children were small, I found that the previous user of the bathroom had finished a roll of toilet paper without replacing it. Unfortunately, I discovered this at an inopportune time. I felt like launching a full-scale investigation and then punishing the perpetrator. I was angry.

But something inside me whispered that there was a better way. How could I accuse and humiliate the people I loved most?

So I called the whole family—all five of us—together into the small bathroom. Then I announced that we had a serious problem. Someone had finished the roll of paper without replacing it. So we would be instituting a new policy. All toilet paper would be stored in a locked closet in the hallway. Paper would only be issued after completing a form in triplicate accounting for each square of paper that was requested.

The children laughed at me. I laughed at me. They got the point without any investigation, accusation, or rancor. Truly a soft approach was better than a hard one. It made the children more mindful of their civic responsibility while preserving our loving relationship.

Very often we want to help our children act better, but then we often set a terrible example of immature rant. Surely there is a better way. Often, humor is not a bad substitute for anger—as long as no one is hurt or humiliated.

I read a story of a teenager who had just learned to drive. She regularly begged for opportunities to drive the family. Once, during a family vacation, her father allowed her to drive on a long, straight stretch of highway. She was in heaven . . . until. Suddenly there was a turn in the road. Caught by surprise, she swung too wide and ran into a service station's sign. She stopped the car and braced herself for a lecture.

Her father, always mindful of his children's feelings, was quiet for some time. Then he turned to the rest of the family in the backseat and said, "As long as we're stopped here, does anybody need to use the rest room?" I suspect that this teenager loved her father for his kindness.

It is important that family laughter not be corrosive or sarcastic. We must never laugh at a family member's pain. But there will be times when laughing together will help the family draw closer together. Kindness and happiness are the lubricants of positive family life.

Reflection

Think of a time when you have used humor instead of anger. How did it feel? What helped you get there? How can you get there again? How can you use that strategy more often and effectively?

Applying this Strategy

☐ I don't think this will work for me.

☐ This is something I am already good at and use regularly to good effect.

☐ This is something I haven't tried but would like to try.

> Next time [insert your parenting dilemma] happens, I'm going to try [insert your personal solution that applies this strategy].
>
>> Write a plan.
>>
>> Visualize yourself doing it.

☐ This is something I have tried but need to practice.

> Next time [insert your parenting dilemma] happens, I'm going to try [insert your personal solution that

applies this strategy].

   Write a plan.

   Visualize yourself doing it.

Notes on progress: _____

_____

_____

_____

_____

4.

Look into the Child's Heart

Very often we judge children's behaviors based on their effects on us. If their actions (or inactions) irritate me, then the children are malicious—or at least careless and irresponsible. They are deliberately trying to make me crazy!

This is much like blaming my extra weight on the fat calories in Reese's peanut butter cups. How much sense would it make to sue the manufacturers of Reese's for making their candy too delectable? Their recipe is not a carefully devised conspiracy against my weight. It is my lack of moderation (or excess of enthusiasm) that is my enemy.

Likewise when a child forgets to close the door, turn off the lights, or to keep cookies out of the living room, they are generally not making a concerted effort to make us poor or crazy. They are probably being children. (By the way, do we sometimes take cookies in the living room or fail to turn off the lights?)

Children's motives are much like ours—only probably a little purer. They are trying to find ways to get their needs met and enjoy life. They probably even want to do what's right as much as they can.

Sometimes their mistakes are simply the result of not knowing better, or being tired, or feeling thwarted and frustrated. To treat them harshly for their humanness is counterproductive.

So the wrath we aim at them is probably unnecessary and unhelpful. We can scald them with our unhappiness and we will all be the poorer.

Jeffrey Holland, a former university president, told a poignant story of overreaction:

Early in our married life my young family and I were laboring through graduate school at a university in New England. I was going to school full-time and teaching half-time. We had two small children then, with little money and lots of pressures.

One evening I came home from long hours at school, feeling the weight of the world on my shoulders. Everything seemed to be especially demanding and discouraging and dark. I wondered if the dawn would ever come. Then, as I walked into our small student apartment, there was an unusual silence in the room.

"What's the trouble?" I asked.

"Matthew has something he wants to tell you," my wife said.

"Matt, what do you have to tell me?" He was quietly playing with his toys in the corner of the room, trying very hard not to hear me. "Matt," I said a little louder, "do you have something to tell me?"

He stopped playing, but for a moment didn't look up. Then these two enormous, tear-filled brown eyes turned toward me, and with the pain only a five-year-old can know, he said, "I didn't mind Mommy tonight, and I spoke back to her." With that he burst into tears, and his entire little body shook with grief. A childish mistake had been noted, a painful confession had been offered, the growth of a five-year-old was continuing, and loving peace could have been wonderfully underway.

Everything might have been just terrific—except for me. If you can imagine such an idiotic thing, I lost my temper.

It wasn't that I lost it with Matt—it was with a hundred and one other things on my mind; but he didn't know that, and I wasn't disciplined enough to admit it. He got the whole load of bricks.

I told him how disappointed I was and how much more I thought I could have expected from him. Then I did what I had never done before in his life—I told him that he was to go straight to bed and that I would not be in to say his prayers with him or to tell him a bedtime story. Muffling his sobs, he obediently went to his bedside, where he knelt—alone—to say his prayers. Then he stained his little pillow with tears his father should have been wiping away.[14]

When we know we are tired, we should be especially cautious about our reactions—and over-reactions. In all cases we should look on children not as annoying people who are tormenting us deliberately, but as children who are doing the best they know how to do.

Reflection

Think of a time when you have looked into your child's heart and intentions. How did it feel? What helped you get there? How can you get there again? How can you make that experience more common for you?

Applying this Strategy

☐ I don't think this will work for me.
☐ This is something I am already good at and use regularly to good effect.
☐ This is something I haven't tried but would like to try.

   Next time [insert your parenting dilemma] happens,
   I'm going to try [insert your personal solution that

applies this strategy].

  Write a plan.

  Visualize yourself doing it.

☐ This is something I have tried but need to practice.

  Next time [insert your parenting dilemma] happens,
  I'm going to try [insert your personal solution that
  applies this strategy].

  Write a plan.

  Visualize yourself doing it.

Notes on progress: _____

_____

_____

_____

_____

5.

Look on Them with Compassion

Anger is no friend to compassion. As soon as anger possesses our soul, we start seeing everything the offender says or does as further insult or wrongdoing.

As Jonathan Haidt, the eminent psychologist observes: "Judgmentalism is indeed a disease of the mind: it leads to anger, torment, and conflict. . . . Violations of *should* statements are the major causes of anger and resentment. [He] advises empathy: In conflict, look at the world from your opponent's point of view, and you'll see that she is not entirely crazy."[15]

We can remove wrath from family relationships by looking on each other with compassion. Of course it is best to cultivate the compassion before the anger gets hold of us.

When our daughter Emily was in kindergarten, she and a neighbor friend named Donna often went across the street to the school playground to kick a ball and swing on the swing set. One day as the two girls left our house and headed to the playground, Emily stopped at curbside and Donna dashed into the street. A slow-moving car was unable to stop and hit Donna sending her skidding and finally sprawling on the pavement. She lay in the street frightened and pained.

What is the right response to Donna's pain? Would it make sense to approach her and remind her of our oft-repeated and wise counsel to look both ways before crossing the street? Would it make sense to tell her that maybe she needed a time-out to reflect on her carelessness? Would we ground her or demand that she apologize to the frightened driver?

No! Such callousness is akin to abuse. We would go to Donna and offer words of love and assurance even as we helped her get comfortable. We would call for appropriate medical care. We would do anything we could to help her feel safe and to start the healing process.

Far more often than we realize, our children are injured by painful encounters with life. They come home bruised, skinned, and bleeding. We adults almost surely do not realize how often they feel frightened and wounded. If we try to understand their pains and challenges, we are likely to look upon them with compassion rather than judgment and impatience.

When our children are injured by unkind words from classmates, rejection by friends, stinging criticism from teachers—whatever the source of the injury—we can respond with compassion.

Haim Ginott tells a great story that illustrates the role of compassion. He tells of 5-year-old Bruce who, with his mother, was making a welcome-to-kindergarten visit to the school. Bruce looked at the drawings on the wall and asked loudly, "Who made these ugly pictures?"

Mom was humiliated by her son's rudeness. She shot at him: "It's not nice to call the pictures ugly when they are so pretty."

The teacher understood Bruce's real question. She smiled and said, "In here you don't have to paint pretty pictures. You can paint mean pictures if you feel like it."

Bruce smiled. Perhaps he had wondered how little boys who don't draw very well are treated in this classroom.

Some minutes later, Bruce picked up a broken toy truck and asked demandingly, "Who broke this fire engine?"

Mother was again mortified. "What difference does it make to you who broke it? You don't know anyone here."

But Bruce wasn't trying to solve a crime. He wanted to know what happened to boys who break toys.

The teacher seemed to understand that motive in Bruce, for her answer radiated compassion: "Toys are for playing. Sometimes they get broken. It happens."

Bruce seemed to relax. He had learned vital lessons about the kindergarten he would soon enter. "This grown-up is pretty nice. She does not get angry quickly, even when a picture comes out ugly or a toy is broken. I don't have to be afraid. It is safe to stay here."

Bruce launched his kindergarten experience feeling safe.

When we see one of our children burdened or injured—even if it is due to their own foolishness—we do not ask, "What's wrong with you, Sourpuss?" Instead, we approach with compassion in our words and in our spirit: "Looks like you've had a hard day." We lean into their struggle with our love.

We do not demand that they tell us more than they are ready to share. But we try to remember and be humbled by the challenges of being a child—feeling unskilled and often powerless. We come to them with emotional first aid.

Having compassion on them can prevent us from attacking unhelpfully. It can also help us deal with differences and irritations when we have them. It reminds us that we are all learners in the schoolroom of life.

Reflection

Think of a time when you have looked on your children with compassion. How did it feel? What helped you get there? How can you get there again? How can you make that experience more common for you?

Applying this Strategy

☐ I don't think this will work for me.

☐ This is something I am already good at and use regularly to good effect.

☐ This is something I haven't tried but would like to try.

> Next time [insert your parenting dilemma] happens, I'm going to try [insert your personal solution that applies this strategy].
>
> > Write a plan.
> >
> > Visualize yourself doing it.

☐ This is something I have tried but need to practice.

> Next time [insert your parenting dilemma] happens, I'm going to try [insert your personal solution that applies this strategy].
>
> > Write a plan.
> >
> > Visualize yourself doing it.

Notes on progress: _____

_____

_____

_____

_____

6.

Listen to Their Hearts

When children are struggling with burdens of pain, we are likely to jump in with unhelpful advising. We may even get angry at the behaviors that got them in their fixes. There is a better way to help them heal, honor their agency, and help them learn. One of the most important things we can do is listen with our hearts.

As children are dealing with disappointment or despair, we bring our compassion as an offering. We show our love and dedication by listening with our souls.

For example, imagine your son coming home from school slumping and sullen. My first reaction is probably to blurt out, "What's wrong with you?!"

We can all predict the response. "Nothing!" he will exclaim. The child might add, "Leave me alone," as he sulks his way to his room.

But if we listen to their hearts, we find a better way of responding. We imagine reasons why he might be dragging and we offer, "It looks like you've had a bad day." And we stop. We give him a chance to share as much as he wants to share. We listen to his heart.

Maybe he decides to trust us. "Today on the bus everyone was acting crazy and running around. The bus driver got mad. He stopped the bus and came back and grabbed me and started yelling at me."

A situation like this strains the compassion of the best parents. One parent reaction would be to cajole, "Yeah. Like you didn't do a thing. Just a poor, innocent kid. Why did the bus driver pick on you? What were you doing that made him blame you?"

We all know that this bitter attack will not yield sweet fruit. The child will resolve never to trust us again.

A second parental reaction is to blame the bus driver. "What's wrong with that crazy man? Doesn't he know better than to pick on kids? I'm going to go have some *words* with him!"

A wise parent knows that this reaction is no more helpful than blaming the child. But the need to investigate and blame is very strong in humans. Unfortunately we're not very good at making sense of the evidence. We tend to use all information in service of the conclusions we favor. If I am often irritated with my son, I assume that the bus driver blamed him with good reason, and I look for any hint of corroborating evidence. If I feel that my son is unfairly treated, I look for evidence that the bus driver is nuts. We humans aren't very objective.

We also are not very good at providing emotional first aid. None of the investigating and blaming is useful while our son is injured. Our first duty is to assure his well-being. I try to understand his feelings and minister to his well-being as long as it takes for him to become more peaceful. This is best done with warm compassion and words of understanding.

> "You must have felt humiliated."
> "I bet you felt hurt and angry."
> "You probably wished you could have disappeared."

As we listen to the child's heart, we advance healing. We offer a safe embrace and compassionate words.

Once the child feels peaceful, the next step is surprisingly simple. We draw on the wisdom within the child: "You had a terrible experience today. What can you do to be sure that doesn't happen again?"

The best answers are in your child.

He may say, "I need to settle down on the bus," or "I need to sit next to someone besides Tommy. He always gets me in trouble," or "I probably need to ride my bike to school. I love tormenting the bus driver too much to resist." He has better answers than we could ever dream of.

The same principles apply in any situation that inflicts emotional pain on a child. If my daughter is hurt by the cruelty of a friend, I might respond, "Oh, Darling! That must feel awful!" Then I stop to listen to anything else she wants to say. When she is peaceful, I invite her to think of ways to prevent future problems.

The common parental temptation is to say far too much—to tell about our pains or to give advice. But a good doctor does not start telling his patients about his own assorted aches, pains, and diseases. He doesn't lecture us about being more careful. He focuses on the patient's injury.

Likewise, our focus on the pain cleanses the wound and begins the healing process. Can you think of a time when someone has responded to your pain with words of compassion?

I remember when I was a young school teacher and my father asked me how my teaching was going. I unloaded on him the demands of preparing many subjects, the pressures from administrators and parents, as well as the impossibility of managing so many students. When I finished, I expected my father to say, "What you need to do is . . . " But he didn't. Instead he said with heartfelt compassion, "That must be overwhelming." That was all he said. But I still feel the warmth of his compassion. Dad listened to my heart and offered his compassion.

He gave me that unique gift of empathy. Maybe the gift is powerful in part because it is so rare. Maybe it is powerful because it requires the giver to set aside his own agenda, feelings, and history in order to inhabit the experience of another person.

If we want to help our children learn to settle themselves from feelings of hurt and resentment, we can listen with our hearts. It is far more effective than giving formulaic advice or demanding that they settle down. It is a great gift of love.

Haim Ginott, the great psychologist, tells of a parent who takes his child for ice cream. When asked which flavor he wanted, the child replied, "I want a scoop of every flavor!" This response could tempt any parent to get angry: "Why, you spoiled brat! I offer you a cone and you want the whole creamery!"

The attack would not be helpful. Instead, the parent can listen to his heart. "Wouldn't that be great! Wouldn't you love to have some of every single flavor! Which two flavors would you like to have today?" The limit can be delivered with loving empathy.

Reflection

Think of a time when you have listened to your child's heart. How did it feel? What helped you get there? How can you get there again? How can you make that experience more common for you?

Applying this Strategy

- ☐ I don't think this will work for me.
- ☐ This is something I am already good at and use regularly to good effect.
- ☐ This is something I haven't tried but would like to try.
    Next time [insert your parenting dilemma] happens, I'm going to try [insert your personal solution that applies this strategy].
        Write a plan.
        Visualize yourself doing it.
- ☐ This is something I have tried but need to practice.

Next time [insert your parenting dilemma] happens,
I'm going to try [insert your personal solution that
applies this strategy].

> Write a plan.
> Visualize yourself doing it.

Notes on progress: _____

_____

_____

_____

_____

7.

Choose Peace

A mother once asked me what she should do about her 4-year-old daughter who had scratched a neighbor's child. The mother wanted to be sure that her daughter got the message: "Your behavior is not acceptable. You must never scratch anyone."

I asked for more information about the incident. The 4-year-old had been playing with her 6-year-old sister and the sister's friend while Mom was preparing dinner. (A sensitive parent sees trouble coming already. Older children are often not very gracious toward younger children who want to play with them.)

As they were playing, the younger child got upset and scratched her sister's friend. I asked the mother how she dealt with it. "I scratched my little girl and then I locked her in her room and told her she could not come out for three days." The mother explained, "I wanted her to learn a lesson."

I think the little girl learned a lesson—but probably not the one Mom intended. The child probably learned that her world is a crazy, tumultuous place. She learned to feel afraid and lonely. She learned that her world is not a safe place.

It was noteworthy that the mother in describing the problem had not mentioned the stresses in their family life that may have impacted the girl's behavior. The dad was overwhelmed with a work project and was working long hours. Mom had started a new job with new pressures and extra hours for training. To accommodate her mother's schedule, the little girl had been moved to a new child care center where she had no friends. And, at the time of the incident, the girls were hungry and tired with one younger child being treated like a plague.

None of these factors justify scratching. But they help us understand the little girl. I asked the mom if her girl scratched often. "No. Maybe once before." The girl was not a serial scratcher.

When the mother asked me what she might have done differently, I tried to imagine the little girl's life. The best solution grows best in the soil of understanding. How might that little girl feel amid the tumult of Mom and Dad's hectic schedules and her own new care setting?

I suggested that the little girl probably needed help finding other ways to express her frustration. In fact, Mom might help her get peaceful by sitting with her little girl in a rocking chair. Mom might calm herself even as she calmed her little girl. When both were peaceful, Mom might offer sympathy and help her daughter learn new ways.

"You must have been very upset today." Mom listens and empathizes. "What a hard day! Did the scratching help you get what you wanted?" Mom listens some more. "Is there anything you could have done differently?" Mom coaches her girl to better ways.

Peace is a better soil for growing children than anger is.

Reflection

Think of a time when you have chosen peace. How did it feel? What helped you get there? How can you get there again? How can you make that experience more common for you?

Applying this Strategy

☐ I don't think this will work for me.
☐ This is something I am already good at and use regularly to good effect.

☐ This is something I haven't tried but would like to try.

 Next time [insert your parenting dilemma] happens, I'm going to try [insert your personal solution that applies this strategy].

  Write a plan.

  Visualize yourself doing it.

☐ This is something I have tried but need to practice.

 Next time [insert your parenting dilemma] happens, I'm going to try [insert your personal solution that applies this strategy].

  Write a plan.

  Visualize yourself doing it.

Notes on progress: _____

_____

_____

_____

_____

8.

Get Their Side of the Story

Turning again to the wisdom of psychologist Jonathan Haidt:

> Recent psychological research has uncovered the mental mechanisms that make us so good at seeing the slightest speck in our neighbor's eye, and so bad at seeing the log in our own. If you know what your mind is up to, and why you so easily see the world through a distorting lens of good and evil, you can take steps to reduce your self-righteousness. You can thereby reduce the frequency of conflicts with others who are equally convinced of their righteousness.[16]

> By seeing the log in your own eye you can become less biased, less moralistic, and therefore less inclined toward argument and conflict.[17]

All of us are unable to see objectively because our own experience blocks our understanding of others' experience. Our own confidence that we are right and our children are just making excuses only worsens the situation.

On one occasion my family and I were planning to go visit a friend who had suffered some major setbacks. We made a point of telling the children to be home at a specific time and were quite emphatic about it.

At the appointed time, however, Emily was missing and could not be found. She had gone to play with Betsy, but the two girls had gone on a walk and had not returned. As we waited at home, I stewed. I reflected on other times that Emily had been late. I fretted that we would not be able to visit our friend as a whole family. I built quite a case against her. Emily's carelessness had robbed us of an important opportunity as a family.

When we could wait no longer, the rest of us went to visit the friend. When we returned home, Emily was there looking very sheepish. My tirade was well-prepared and fully-rehearsed. Fortunately, I had just enough good sense to ask Emily to explain her absence at the appointed time.

She apologized. She said that she and Betsy had gone to see Millie Haws, a widow who lived down the street. They had visited for a while and then told Millie that they needed to go. But Millie begged them to hear just one more story. They fidgeted and fretted but did not know how to break free from Millie's story in a polite way.

I might have lectured Emily about assertiveness and responsibility, but I, like her, had been caught more than once in Millie's magical storytelling. All I could do was sigh in sympathy and thank Emily for the compassion that took her to visit Millie in the first place.

Each of us constructs stories to explain what we see others do. We take what we know of the facts and personalities and we put them together in a coherent manner. There is only one problem. There are vast gaps in our knowledge of facts and our assessments of other people's character. That is why it is so important to forego dogmatism in favor of humility. That is why it is so important to hear their side of the story. "It is a mighty thin pancake that does not have two sides," said Mary Christensen.[18]

As Haidt observed, "by seeing the log in your own eye you can become less biased, less moralistic, and therefore less inclined toward argument and conflict."[19] Two can see better than one. In fact, our children know far more about their lives than we do. When we get their side of the story, we can act in ways that are wiser and more helpful. We can become soft-spoken parents.

Reflection

Think of a time when you have gotten their side of the story. How did it feel? What helped you get there? How can you get there again? How can you make that experience more common for you?

Applying this Strategy

☐ I don't think this will work for me.

☐ This is something I am already good at and use regularly to good effect.

☐ This is something I haven't tried but would like to try.

    Next time [insert your parenting dilemma] happens, I'm going to try [insert your personal solution that applies this strategy].

        Write a plan.

        Visualize yourself doing it.

☐ This is something I have tried but need to practice.

    Next time [insert your parenting dilemma] happens, I'm going to try [insert your personal solution that applies this strategy].

        Write a plan.

        Visualize yourself doing it.

Notes on progress: _____

_____

_____

_____

_____

9.

Walk in Their Shoes

It is very hard for adults to understand what life is like for children. We have changed so slowly and so completely from childhood to adulthood that we may not even realize how different our experience is from theirs.

For example, we might not guess that prominent among children's concerns is the dread that they might wet their pants in school. That might seem silly to adults. But maybe we forget that they must still get permission to go to the restroom. Children often feel quite powerless in their lives.

Also they remember times when they (or classmates) have had accidents. And they remember the humiliation of being teased over those accidents.

Most of us have forgotten many of the challenges of adolescence. Teens are just learning to think about thinking. They are learning to think about how other people think about them. It can be a very confusing—albeit necessary—development.

We sometimes talk about adolescent egocentrisms. For example, teens tend to feel as if people are always watching them. They also yearn to be heroic. And they often believe that they are invincible. As a result of these ways of thinking, teens may be very sensitive, they may take an inordinate amount of time getting ready for school, and they may ruminate about things that their classmates say to them or about them.

It may seem to adults that teens are irrational and oversensitive. But this stage of making sense of their inner world and their social world is as important as a one-year-old learning to walk or a two-year-old stringing words together to express ideas. It is a normal and important part of development.

Do you remember feeling painfully self-conscious as a child? Do you remember wondering what people thought of you? Do you remember blushing with embarrassment over things you said? Do you remember being made fun of by classmates? If so, you may have the humility to understand your child.

Of course each child is different from us in important ways. Our experiences, therefore, only provide us needed humility; they do not give us the answers for our children's challenges.

With humility in place, we can study our children. We can notice what they love and what they are afraid of. We can notice what they enjoy and what they dread. Our objective is to walk in their shoes so that we can better understand their view of the world. If we do this with genuine humility, we can then help them navigate lives.

My wife, Nancy, and I used to go out to dinner occasionally so that we could discuss each of our children. Nancy would ask how we might help one child make more friends or deal with a difficult experience. I offered possibilities. Because of her sensitivity to the children, she knew which suggestions fitted them best. Together we made plans to support and help each child in the way that would work for them.

Anjelica Huston reports that when she was young she made some negative comment about Vincent van Gogh at the dinner table. She said somewhat flippantly that she didn't like his work. Her father, the famous movie director John Huston, exploded: "You don't like van Gogh? Then name six of his paintings and tell me why you don't like them." When she couldn't, he commanded her: "Leave the room, and until you know what you're talking about, don't come back with your opinions to the dinner table."

Harsh attacks do not humble and they do not inform. They create resentment. John Huston was not in a debate with an art critic. He was mentoring a child. A parent's job is to educate and enlarge a child's sensibilities.

John Huston might have considered forms of art he didn't enjoy. Then he might understand that van Gogh simply did not speak to his daughter. Contrast Huston's harsh response with the teaching response described by Haim Ginott:

> When Clara, age fourteen, criticized modern painting, mother did not dispute her opinion. Nor did she condemn her taste.
>
> Mother: You don't like abstract art?
>
> Clara: I sure don't. It's ugly.
>
> Mother: You prefer representational art?
>
> Clara: What's that?
>
> Mother: You like it when a house looks like a house, and a tree like a tree and a person like a person.
>
> Clara: Yes.
>
> Mother: Then you like representational art.
>
> Clara: Imagine that. All my life I liked representational art and didn't know it.

Clara's mother worked with daughter's feelings and preferences in order to educate her. And in the process she showed both respect and affection.

You know the old saying: We cannot understand someone until we have walked a mile in their shoes. That is certainly true of understanding our children. When we understand the landscape of their lives—their hopes, anxieties, preferences, dreams, and monsters—we are less likely to get angry or impatient with them. We are more likely to help them find their way to happy adulthoods.

Reflection

Think of a time when you have walked in your children's shoes—when you have connected their experience with your own. How did it feel? What helped you get there? How can you get there again? How can you make that experience more common for you?

Applying this Strategy

☐ I don't think this will work for me.

☐ This is something I am already good at and use regularly to good effect.

☐ This is something I haven't tried but would like to try.

> Next time [insert your parenting dilemma] happens, I'm going to try [insert your personal solution that applies this strategy].

> > Write a plan.

> > Visualize yourself doing it.

☐ This is something I have tried but need to practice.

> Next time [insert your parenting dilemma] happens, I'm going to try [insert your personal solution that applies this strategy].

> > Write a plan.

> > Visualize yourself doing it.

Notes on progress: _____

_____

_____

_____

_____

10.

Put Off 'til Tomorrow What
Shouldn't Be Said Today

I stood in a bank lobby talking with a friend. We had talked for some time when the friend's teenage son approached. He waited anxiously for a few minutes looking for an opportunity to interrupt. His father ignored him even though he was clearly aware of his presence. Finally, the boy broke into our conversation, "Dad, I've got to go to work . . ." The man turned to his son and exploded, "Why are you so rude! What's wrong with you? Don't you have any manners?"

I tend to think of manners as a two-way street. The son had clearly tried to wait for an opportune moment to interrupt. The dad might have excused himself from our conversation for a moment. (Or, if I had had greater presence of mind, I might have said, "It appears that your son needs you. I'll fill out my deposit slip while you talk.")

Instead, a well-intended father was trying to teach his son patience by making him wait and humility by humiliating him. Neither worked. The boy only learned that his father did not care about his feelings.

Sometimes a clever observation is exploding to get out of us. We're tempted to point out that our children brought their suffering on themselves because of their bad decisions. Or when they seem cocky, we're tempted to cut them down to size with a sarcastic remark. Or maybe we're mad because we've been stupid and we'd rather blame the child than take personal responsibility.

As the indignation surges, a voice inside of us gently reminds us that we should not make our terse observation. As the proverb says, it is never a good idea to burn a cathedral just to fry an egg, even when we are terribly hungry. To torch a relationship in order to feel clever or exonerated is equally shortsighted.

Torn between the temptation to correct, level, or humble the child and the invitation to kindness and helpfulness, many of us gag the angel and speak for the devil. That's where the impulsive energy is. It is so much *easier* to do what comes naturally. (Or so it seems.)

Sometimes we imagine that it is our duty to correct error in our children. It is our job as parents to let them know when they are out of line. We need to humble them. We don't dare stifle that message and mission.

A wise voice within us encourages us *not* to speak when we feel frustrated and judgmental. That is why we should often put off until tomorrow what we shouldn't say today. If we make an agreement with ourselves to never speak in haste or anger, we honor the better angels of our nature.

As we allow time to settle our souls, we can see the irritation in perspective. We should not call in a full armada to quell a tempest in a teapot. So, when we are calm enough and balanced enough to see our children as good people doing their best, then maybe we can be helpful.

Many years ago, as I wrestled with proper ways to correct our children, I learned an ironic principle: I only have the right to correct those I love. Any time I am feeling impatient or judgmental, I am not prepared to correct.

The irony in this principle is that, when I am wholeheartedly loving my child, the urge to correct evaporates. Or, if there is still some need to correct, it is done in a spirit that is helpful rather than punitive.

So, rather than let untamed correction spill out of us, we can make the resolve to hold our tongues when we are upset. Then we can use the time that is granted us to regain the balanced perspective. When we are feeling loving and appreciative, the message we deliver is likely to be helpful. And a great number of irritations really don't need to even be discussed. We merely need Tums and time.

Reflection

Think of a time when you have put off making the cutting remark. How did it feel to triumph over the unkind remark? What helped you get there? How can you get there again? How can you make that experience more common for you?

Applying this Strategy

- [ ] I don't think this will work for me.
- [ ] This is something I am already good at and use regularly to good effect.
- [ ] This is something I haven't tried but would like to try.
      Next time [insert your parenting dilemma] happens, I'm going to try [insert your personal solution that applies this strategy].
      Write a plan.
      Visualize yourself doing it.
- [ ] This is something I have tried but need to practice.
      Next time [insert your parenting dilemma] happens, I'm going to try [insert your personal solution that applies this strategy].
      Write a plan.
      Visualize yourself doing it.

Notes on progress: _____

_____

_____

_____

_____

11.

When Necessary, Correct Children with Wisdom, Precision, and Gentleness

How often are our reproofs motivated by helpful intent? In over three decades of parenting, I can think of very few times when my reproving was motivated by noble purposes. Usually I was merely venting my spleen. Or sometimes I was looking for a scapegoat with whom to share my unhappiness.

Imagine that a law enforcement officer comes to your door early one Saturday morning. He tells you that your son has been out with his friends the night before and has blown up Mrs. Jones' mailbox with a bunch of firecrackers.

You have several options. You could call him to the door and have him face the police alone. You can burst into his room and read him the riot act. Or you could teach with wisdom, precision, and gentleness, before you invite him to work things out with the police.

I favor the third option. Loving parents are the best people to teach their children. So imagine that you tell the officer that you would like to visit with your son and that you will bring him to the station later in the day.

Then you go to your son's room. "Son, a police officer was just here to see you." A simple statement such as this almost guarantees your son's attention.

The next step is vitally important. We can accuse, "What were you thinking? I thought you were a smarter kid! Do you know what trouble you're in?" Or we can connect, "Let me see if I know what happened last night. I'm guessing that you and your friends were out having fun and you saw Mrs. Jones' mailbox. You thought it would be much improved by some firecrackers. Am I close?"

When we start by assuming that our children do what they do for reasons that make sense to them, we honor the social contract. We honor the connection that should bind children to parents and parents to children. We strengthen our bond.

Your son may admit the pyrotechnical fun. Now the door is open for teaching. You might say, "Son, the government considers that mailboxes belong to them. They get quite upset when someone messes with them."

Your son may protest. "That's stupid." We don't have to argue the point. "I'm not sure if I understand the law. But I know that the police get very upset when fireworks and mailboxes get together."

There are primarily two kinds of teaching: teaching the mind and teaching the heart. Let's start with the mind.

"So Mrs. Jones has a problem. She does not have a mailbox."

Your son might sigh, "We can get her a new mailbox."

"That would be great! Thank you, Son. There is another problem that's harder to deal with."

Your son looks at you quizzically: "What's that?"

"You and I probably don't understand what life is like for Mrs. Jones. She has been a widow for a few years. She lives alone. I wonder what last night was like for her."

If you're lucky, your son will be thinking and feeling. So we continue, putting emphasis on educating the heart. "I'm guessing that she felt very vulnerable. She heard scuffling on the porch and then she heard explosions. She may have worried about her safety. She may have wondered if someone was going to hurt her. She may not feel safe in her own home."

If we are lucky, the message will have touched your son's heart. He may be feeling very concerned for Mrs. Jones. "I didn't think of that. What can I do?"

"Can you think of anything that would make her feel more safe?"

"Maybe my friends and I could visit her and apologize. Maybe we could explain that we didn't want to hurt her. Maybe we could offer to help her look after her place."

That would be a payday for a parent! A youthful mistake had been acknowledged, a mind had been educated, a heart had been softened, a plan had been developed. Those are the outcomes we seek as parents.

Before taking our son to his interview with the police, we might coach him on working with the police. Take their concern seriously. Acknowledge your mistake. Take responsibility for setting things right. Offer to accompany him. (Sometimes a calm parent can coach a teen and an officer into a reasonable understanding.)

I should frankly acknowledge that the story above is invented. Usually parents never learn about their teens' misdeeds. When they do, they are likely to set off their own fireworks. Yet when we find a way to correct with wisdom, precision, and gentleness, our efforts will be richly rewarded.

Reflection

Think of a time when you have corrected with wisdom, precision, and gentleness. How did it feel? What helped you get there? How can you get there again? How can you make that experience more common for you?

Applying this Strategy

☐ I don't think this will work for me.

☐ This is something I am already good at and use regularly to good effect.

☐ This is something I haven't tried but would like to try.

> Next time [insert your parenting dilemma] happens, I'm going to try [insert your personal solution that applies this strategy].
>
>> Write a plan.
>>
>> Visualize yourself doing it.

☐ This is something I have tried but need to practice.

> Next time [insert your parenting dilemma] happens, I'm going to try [insert your personal solution that applies this strategy].
>
>> Write a plan.
>>
>> Visualize yourself doing it.

Notes on progress: _____

_____

_____

_____

_____

12.

Take a Mental Vacation

When something bothers us, we humans often choose to be mad. We choose recreational anger. It can be quite energizing to feel that something is wrong and to lead the charge against an enemy.

Research on close relationships shows that taking time out from our fights is not useful *if* we keep up our distress-maintaining cognitions—in other words, if we keep thinking in ways that keep us mad.

If we impose a time-out on a lecture or argument with one of our children and we go out in the backyard and, while weeding the flower beds, we build our case against the child, we are not using the time-out effectively.

When we take a break from a family battle, it may be quite helpful to take a mental break as well as a physical break. We can take time to enjoy nature. We can read something enriching. Maybe we even pray. We cannot think right while feeling wrong.

The insightful psychologist Jonathan Haidt suggests a wise exercise that provides a mental vacation from our anger and accusation:

> Try this now: Think of a recent interpersonal conflict with someone you care about and then find one way in which your behavior was not exemplary. Maybe you did something insensitive (even if you had a right to do it), or hurtful (even if you meant well), or inconsistent with your principles (even though you can readily justify it).
>
> When you find a fault in yourself it will hurt, briefly, but if you keep going and acknowledge the fault, you

are likely to be rewarded with a flash of pleasure that is mixed, oddly, with a hint of pride. It is the pleasure of taking responsibility for your own behavior. It is the feeling of honor.

Finding fault with yourself is also the key to overcoming the hypocrisy and judgmentalism that damage so many valuable relationships. The instant you see some contribution you made to a conflict, your anger softens— maybe just a bit, but enough that you might be able to acknowledge some merit on the other side.

You can still believe you are right and the other person is wrong, but if you move to believing that you are *mostly* right, and your opponent is *mostly* wrong, you have the basis for an effective and nonhumiliating apology. You can take a small piece of the disagreement and say, "I should not have done X, and I can see why you felt Y."[20]

When we see our own contribution to a problem, we are better able to be helpful. We remove accusation, misunderstanding, resentment, and hostility. We see lovingly, compassionately, hopefully, and helpfully.

We cannot think right about each other when we are rehearsing each other's faults. So we interrupt our thoughts in order to see each other with kindness and pure knowledge. When we find ourselves filled with irritation or accusation, we can take a break—a mental vacation. During that break, we can fill our souls with gratitude for life's riches, and we can seek to see each other in kind, appreciative ways.

Reflection

Think of a time when you have taken a mental vacation that helped you get things in perspective. How did it feel? What helped you get there?

How can you get there again? How can you make that experience more common for you?

Applying this Strategy

☐ I don't think this will work for me.

☐ This is something I am already good at and use regularly to good effect.

☐ This is something I haven't tried but would like to try.

    Next time [insert your parenting dilemma] happens, I'm going to try [insert your personal solution that applies this strategy].

        Write a plan.

        Visualize yourself doing it.

☐ This is something I have tried but need to practice.

    Next time [insert your parenting dilemma] happens, I'm going to try [insert your personal solution that applies this strategy].

        Write a plan.

        Visualize yourself doing it.

Notes on progress: _____

_____

_____

_____

_____

13.

Breathe Deeply

A man was guiding several youngsters through the various exhibits in a museum. He obviously was impatient with the side trips and slow pace of the children. He blurted out, "Hurry up! If you stop to look at stuff, we won't get to see anything."

The man may have needed to take a deep breath and reset his internal clock to youthful-exploration pace. If we are to be effective parents for our children, we may need to do the same.

I remember looking out my office window one day to see a mother unload her little girl from the car. As the mother rounded up her purse from the car, the little girl toddled to the sidewalk where she discovered a line of ants busily at work. I watched with interest as the mother caught up to her daughter. I expected Mom to give a cursory nod to ant watching before dragging her little girl to their appointment. She didn't. Instead Mom knelt with her girl and watched the ants. They talked about the ants. They studied the ants. For several minutes they became a team of naturalists. After several minutes, the daughter was ready to move on. That was a mama who knew how to enjoy a breath of life.

Some people use a mindfulness of breathing as part of meditation. It can turn us from fretting to relaxing. It can help us resist anger.

But unless you meditate—or have asthma—you probably don't think about breathing very much. It just happens. We take it for granted. But we can move from toe-tapping impatience to breath-savoring peacefulness.

Every time we inhale we might be grateful for the gift of life—and maybe even children. Every time we exhale we might remember that, at our very best, we are still children ourselves—that we draw on the patience of many others.

When we feel the rising tide of anger in our souls, we might turn our attention from organizing our complaints to enjoying each breath.

My friend William is a good example of humble gratitude. William was born with muscular dystrophy and a variety of mental diseases including schizophrenia and bipolar disorder. He had also made some mistakes that put him in jail for a time. One day Nancy and I visited him in the state mental hospital. We asked him how he was doing. He said something I'll always remember: "I can breathe—and it doesn't get any better than that."

William, with all his challenges, reminds me that I can be grateful for the simplest blessings. When I am consciously mindful and thankful for the gift of breath, among a million other blessings, I'm a little less likely to dump a load of unhappiness on a struggling child.

So, let's breathe deeply.

Reflection

Think of a time when you have taken time to relax, to breathe deeply, and to be consciously grateful. How did it feel? What helped you get there? How can you get there again? How can you make that experience more common for you?

Applying this Strategy

☐ I don't think this will work for me.
☐ This is something I am already good at and use regularly to good effect.
☐ This is something I haven't tried but would like to try.

Next time [insert your parenting dilemma] happens, I'm going to try [insert your personal solution that applies this strategy].

> Write a plan.

> Visualize yourself doing it.

☐ This is something I have tried but need to practice.

> Next time [insert your parenting dilemma] happens, I'm going to try [insert your personal solution that applies this strategy].

> > Write a plan.

> > Visualize yourself doing it.

Notes on progress: _____

_____

_____

_____

_____

14.

Just Listen

We humans are like writers of fiction. We take life experiences and form them into stories. But the stories are never objective. We write to make a point. We color every story with our point of view.

Social psychologists have observed that we humans are not very objective—even at our best: "Instead of a naïve scientist entering the environment in search of the truth, we find the rather unflattering picture of a charlatan trying to make the data come out in a manner most advantageous to his or her already-held theories."[21]

We color our stories with our own favored colors. Yet there is more bad news. Each of us thinks our view is the only right one.

> Each of us thinks we see the world directly, as it really is. We further believe that the facts as we see them are there for all to see, therefore others should agree with us. If they don't agree, it follows either that they have not yet been exposed to the relevant facts or else that they are blinded by their interests and ideologies. If I could nominate one candidate for "biggest obstacle to world peace and social harmony," it would be naïve realism because it is so easily ratcheted up from the individual to the group level.[22]

The only way you can hope to make sense of someone else's experience is by seeing as they see. Unless we set aside our own assumptions, interpretations, and judgments, we cannot help a struggling child. We will be imposing our interpretations on their very different experiences.

If we remove our quirky lenses, and just observe, we may learn a lot. We may find that the children who have drawn our ire are just little strugglers doing the best they know how. They may feel confused, lonely, and sad. They may not know how to do any better.

How many times have all of us looked on friends and children and filtered their stories through our own values and expectations?

Author Carol Lynn Pearson shared the following experience:

> I can remember many occasions when my perception has crumbled and a glimpse inside has wiped away judgment. During my college years I looked at a fellow student, whom I will call Roy, in amazement. Where did he get such a gigantic ego? His need to be recognized and praised was never ending. Every conversation he had with anyone always centered on his recent triumphs and the projects he was now involved in that would ensure his fame. He was underappreciated and let everyone know it. His name became a joke. We had him pegged as an obnoxious egomaniac who blew his own horn from morning until night.
>
> One day I learned that one of my friends knew his family. She began to tell me some things. "Roy's father was an alcoholic. Did you know that?"
>
> "No, I didn't."
>
> "Oh, yes. He made their life just miserable. He was a crazy man. Once, when Roy was about five he walked in the kitchen and saw his father attempting to kill his mother. It was a terrible scene and Roy was there to watch it all."

The tremor was instant. All my perceptions, all my judgment shattered, and I saw past the facade in the reality. I saw past the obnoxious adult to the traumatized little boy that I wanted to take in my arms and comfort. I never looked at Roy the same again. I knew his secret, or of his secrets, and I understood.[23]

Having spent a lifetime learning how to interpret what we see and hear, we now are invited to turn off the interpretation. Instead of re-writing others' stories with our interpretations, we listen carefully to hear their stories, their hearts, their hopes. This isn't easy.

I think this is sage counsel: "Resolve to be tender with the young, compassionate with the aged, sympathetic with the striving and tolerant of the weak and the strong. Sometime in life you will have been all of these."[24]

Reflection

Think of a time when you have listened carefully to what one of your children is telling you with his or her words and actions. How did it feel? What helped you get there? How can you get there again? How can you make that experience more common for you?

Applying this Strategy

☐ I don't think this will work for me.

☐ This is something I am already good at and use regularly to good effect.

☐ This is something I haven't tried but would like to try.

> Next time [insert your parenting dilemma] happens, I'm going to try [insert your personal solution that applies this strategy].
>
> Write a plan.

Visualize yourself doing it.

☐ This is something I have tried but need to practice.

Next time [insert your parenting dilemma] happens, I'm going to try [insert your personal solution that applies this strategy].

Write a plan.

Visualize yourself doing it.

Notes on progress: _____

_____

_____

_____

_____

15.

Be on the Same Team

Humans tend to divide the human race up into teams—often just two teams: Us and Them. There are those we know and like. There are those we mistrust and dislike.

There actually is a systematic bias in the way we see people. Humans tend to blame their own mistakes on their circumstances. "I was under a lot of pressure!" Meanwhile we tend to blame other people's mistakes on their lack of character. "He's not very honest." "She's lazy." Maybe this bias is a result of the fact that we know more about the pressures we face than we know about the pressures that others face.

So, I'm one of the good guys and you're a bad guy. You can imagine the mischief this causes when we divide up *within* families. Maybe I have a hard time with one of the children and I tend to see laziness, meanness, dishonesty, and selfishness in that child. In many cases, that child is much like all other children. In some way, that child bothers me—maybe because he or she reminds me of my own weaknesses. But if I start looking for badness, I will surely find it!

We may not realize how much this way of seeing a person is a choice. We choose to be irritated with something one child does. We choose to wonder about his character. We choose to start looking for more evidence of her badness. We feel justified in our judgment by the new evidence we find.

Our 6-year-old grandson Shad is one of the most energetic boys I know. It is amazing to watch him eat his dinner. He rocks in his chair. He slumps. He taps the table. He twists. He pats the wall. And he does all of this while actually consuming some food.

It is not hard to work up a solid case of irritation with Shad's hyperkinesis. I can sit solemn and glum looking for my next justification to lecture him. Or, in my finer moments, I enjoy his energy. I remember that Shad has a great tenderness. Instead of being irritated, I might be wise enough to talk with Shad about his soccer game or his ziplining. I predict that Shad will be a fine athlete and a hard-working, devoted father.

Irving Becker wisely identified how our choices affect our attitudes toward people: "If you don't like someone, the way he holds his spoon will make you furious; if you do like him, he can turn his plate over into your lap and you won't mind."[25]

So we can choose to be painfully human—chafing over this discontent or that and organizing our complaints—or we can choose to be gracious—looking with compassion, striving to help, acknowledging our own humanness.

Rather than letting differences in preference or style become a source of irritation and judgment, we can make creative use of our differences. For example, rather than reacting to our children's music as if it were the mayhem of a train wreck, we can invite them to teach us about the group, the lyrics, and what they enjoy about it. Or, at least, we can ask them to close the door when they play their stereo.

Instead of seeing the children as aliens sent to torment us, we see them as family members, fellow travelers in the human journey, brothers and sisters. We offer healing kindness and compassion. That is what being on the same team is all about.

Reflection

Think of a time when you have encouraged the sense of being on the same team with your children. How did it feel? What helped you get there? How can you get there again? How can you make that experience more common for you?

Applying this Strategy

☐ I don't think this will work for me.

☐ This is something I am already good at and use regularly to good effect.

☐ This is something I haven't tried but would like to try.

 Next time [insert your parenting dilemma] happens, I'm going to try [insert your personal solution that applies this strategy].

  Write a plan.

  Visualize yourself doing it.

☐ This is something I have tried but need to practice.

 Next time [insert your parenting dilemma] happens, I'm going to try [insert your personal solution that applies this strategy].

  Write a plan.

  Visualize yourself doing it.

Notes on progress: _____

_____

_____

_____

_____

16.

Make Sure Your Actions Match Your Words

Children only learn the meaning of our words by connecting them to our actions. When our words and actions don't match, they believe our actions and ignore our words.

For example, parents all over the world tell their children to put their toys away or they will be sorry. Then we scurry off to talk on the phone, watch TV, or cook dinner. We don't give the toys another thought. Until we trip on them. Then we explode, "I told you to put away your toys!"

But most of the time our children see no clear connection between our words and our actions. It appears that our words are nothing more than our humming dark chords from Beethoven's 9th. There is no evidence that we really care about the toys or their sense of responsibility. Our talk has no meaning for them.

When we get mad, they might say, "Based on experience, I only think you're serious about my toys when you turn red and start to scream. Until then, I assume you are just talking for fun. Let me know when you're really serious."

This lesson is a vital lesson for the soft-spoken parent. We often ask children to do things but we don't send clear messages. We leave them wondering if we mean it. When they don't do what we have asked, we become angry. We wonder, "Why don't they do what we ask?" But our children might ask, "Why do you so often ask me to do things when it is clear that you don't intend to follow up? I believe your actions more than your words."

See if any of these situations seem familiar:

> "If you don't eat your dinner, you can't have dessert."
> They don't eat dinner and they still get dessert.

> "I'm counting to three!" When we get to three, we issue
> a new threat. Finally we scream, "I don't know what I'm
> going to do with you!"

> "Clean up your room or you can't go out to play." We get
> distracted. They go out and play while the room remains
> a wreck.

> "You may not have a candy bar." We get tired of the
> whining, so we provide a candy bar.

Often when our children do not respond to our weak requests, we get mad at the children. Yet we share responsibility. We need to say only those things that we intend to enforce. We should make our actions match our words.

But we don't have to become chronic wailing banshees to be taken seriously. There is a better way. For example, when we ask children to put away toys, we might help them get started. Or we might have an older sibling help them. Or we might take a few minutes to make a game of it with them. Or we can count them as they drop them in the toy box. We can sing a song as we work together. We can let the children know that we were serious about our request *and* we can remain completely pleasant while doing it.

It should be clear that we should not make a rule or request that we do not care enough about to enforce.

My colleague Laura allowed her boys to watch cartoons in the morning only *after* they were fully dressed and ready for school.

Our friend Toni had a rule that the children were not to bring cookies into the living room. When Toni's daughter Julie wandered into the living room bearing a cookie, Mom would invite, "Oh! You want a cookie. Let's go in the kitchen to eat it."

Another parent, Susan, had an agreement with her daughter. She was supposed to practice the piano for thirty minutes before dinner. When the daughter forgot, the dinner was saved until the practicing was completed.

We should only make rules that are important enough to enforce. Some may protest, "But that takes so much time!" I'm guessing that a scientific study would find that parents who make sure that their requests are taken seriously will invest hundreds of hours *less* time over a lifetime than the parents who nag, cajole, and concede. And they will have lower blood pressure and better relationships with their children.

An ounce of prevention is worth a ton of preaching.

Reflection

Think of a time when you have made your actions match your words and have done it in kind ways. How did it feel? What helped you get there? How can you get there again? How can you make that experience more common for you?

Applying this Strategy

- [ ] I don't think this will work for me.
- [ ] This is something I am already good at and use regularly to good effect.
- [ ] This is something I haven't tried but would like to try.
  Next time [insert your parenting dilemma] happens,
  I'm going to try [insert your personal solution that

applies this strategy].

Write a plan.

Visualize yourself doing it.

☐ This is something I have tried but need to practice.

Next time [insert your parenting dilemma] happens, I'm going to try [insert your personal solution that applies this strategy].

Write a plan.

Visualize yourself doing it.

Notes on progress: _____

_____

_____

_____

_____

17.

Blame It on the Rain

A few years ago two dear friends called me from a distant city. Their voices betrayed their exhaustion. "We've had trouble with Breck lately. We don't know what to do. We're desperate. Will you help us?"

The weary parents described the stresses around their recent move to a new city. The dad's new job entailed long hours leaving very little time or energy for his family. The mom was overwhelmed with the demands of the move and organizing the household.

Six-year-old Breck had started acting angry and hostile. Every day he would battle against getting on the bus. He seemed almost to take joy in torturing his mother as she tried to rush him to the school bus that was holding up traffic by fighting with her. "It seems that he is deliberately trying to manipulate me," observed the frustrated mother. "I think he wants to use his power to control the family. He seems to enjoy it."

When the mother asked me if I believed that Breck was trying to manipulate her, my instinctive response was, "No. I know Breck. He is an earnest, sweet, normal boy whose worst fault may be that he is tender and a perfectionist. I think he is saying, 'I am so confused about this move! I like to have some order in my life, but I have been torn away from friends, our old house, familiar routines . . . and now my mom and dad don't even want to snuggle with me at night because they say I need to be grown up. I feel desperately confused and lonely! Please! Please! Someone help me!'"

Seeing Breck as a lonely, confused boy leads to a parenting response very different from the one that would result from seeing him as devious and contrary. Bringing him up in light and truth includes seeing him in the best possible light—as a little boy wanting to be good but feeling very lost, lonely, and overwhelmed.

Rather than accuse, confront, and threaten, parents might respond to the message of pain and confusion that the boy's behavior represents. They can help the troubled boy against their common enemies of confusion, alienation, and fear. His father might say, "Wow! Son, you are really angry. Shall we run around the block together so that you can show me your anger?" Or mother might say, "Son, this all seems so confusing. Can we snuggle together in the rocking chair?" There are probably many more ideas that are still better. And parents are uniquely qualified, based on experience and inspiration, to know what will work with a given child in a specific circumstance. There are many responses that might help the boy deal with his immediate anger and confusion.

Long term solutions to help the boy might include arranging for the mother to volunteer at school so that she could be with her boy during the difficult weeks of transition to a new school. Dad might carve out some time for his son on the weekends. Mom might have the boy stay home from school with her once a week to have time together for a picnic. The family might invite one of Breck's classmates over to play at the house after school to help him build new friendships.

When children cannot find a good way to get their needs met, they may resort to terrorism, not out of spiteful nastiness, but out of desperation. Maybe rather than wanting power over the family, Breck really wanted to feel a little power in his own life. Maybe rather than trying to manipulate and punish the family, he really wanted to feel loved and safe.[26]

That's why I say to blame it on the rain. Think about the rain that is falling in your child's life. Think about the stresses in his or her life. Think about the stresses in the family that might make your child feel anxious or lonely. A move? Health problems? Stress? Money problems?

The bad behavior we see in children is often due to the thunderstorm in their lives. So, blame it on the rain rather than blame it on badness in the child.

Reflection

Think of a time when you have recognized the circumstances that make it hard for your child to be peaceful and loving. Think of a time when you have tried to understand the pressures in your child's life. How did it feel? What helped you get there? How can you get there again? How can you make that experience more common for you?

Applying this Strategy

☐ I don't think this will work for me.

☐ This is something I am already good at and use regularly to good effect.

☐ This is something I haven't tried but would like to try.

> Next time [insert your parenting dilemma] happens, I'm going to try [insert your personal solution that applies this strategy].
>
>> Write a plan.
>> Visualize yourself doing it.

☐ This is something I have tried but need to practice.

> Next time [insert your parenting dilemma] happens, I'm going to try [insert your personal solution that applies this strategy].
>
>> Write a plan.
>> Visualize yourself doing it.

Notes on progress: _____

_____

_____

_____

_____

18.

Reframe the Way You See Them

Our first response to a problem is generally an accusation: "What were you thinking?" "What's wrong with you?" "Why don't you think?"

This is neither motivating nor informative. It tends to lead to hardening of the categories. Soon we begin to see the child as stubborn or willful or contrary, or in some other unflattering way.

Consider Shannon's experience. One evening her mother was expecting company and had been rushing around preparing last-minute details. Mother had snapped at Shannon because she hadn't done her homework or taken her bath. Mom lectured her about responsibility. Then, when Mom walked into the living room, she discovered that Shannon had been trying to help her mother by dusting and polishing the furniture. Mom realized her mistake and hugged her earnest little girl. But company was already arriving and Shannon's surprise was quickly forgotten.

Later that evening, after the company had departed, Mom tucked Shannon into bed. As she turned to leave, she noticed tears forming in Shannon's eyes. "What's the matter, Dear?" She asked. Shannon looked her mother in the eye and asked the question that weighed on her soul. "Mom, why is it that when I do something bad, we talk about it so much? But when I try to do something good, it seems like I'm the only one who remembers?"

Shannon's question challenges all parents. Why do we notice and discuss misdeeds so often while neglecting good intentions and best efforts?

Haim Ginott, the famous child psychologist, recommended that we be advocates for our children. That does not mean that we ignore all their problems and limitations. But it means that we look for the good in them. He said, "Nature always sides with the hidden flaw. [We] have the opposite role: to side with the hidden asset, to minimize children's deficiencies, intensify their experience, and enlarge their lives."[27]

So, when we are tempted to point the accusing finger at our children, we might choose instead to become their advocates. We remember their strengths. We flip weaknesses over to see the strengths on the other side. This is called reframing.

Wally's stubbornness is connected to his strong character. Alan's temper may come from a tender heart that is easily injured. Beth's whining may come from feeling left out when she likes to be included.

Any time we are filled with accusation, we would be wise to turn our backs on negativity and turn toward the light. We use our talents to understand and appreciate our children.

Reflection

Think of a time when you challenged the negative, accusing voice that focuses on the faults of your children. Think of a time when you have replaced accusation with appreciation. How did it feel? What helped you get there? How can you get there again? How can you make that experience more common for you?

Applying this Strategy

☐ I don't think this will work for me.

☐ This is something I am already good at and use regularly to good effect.

☐ This is something I haven't tried but would like to try.

    Next time [insert your parenting dilemma] happens,

    I'm going to try [insert your personal solution that

applies this strategy].

    Write a plan.

    Visualize yourself doing it.

☐ This is something I have tried but need to practice.

    Next time [insert your parenting dilemma] happens, I'm going to try [insert your personal solution that applies this strategy].

    Write a plan.

    Visualize yourself doing it.

Notes on progress: _____

_____

_____

_____

_____

19.

Imagine Yourself Watching a Stage Play

It is easy to get swept up in the drama of our lives so that we can no longer see things as they really are. We become so engaged in playing our part that we see nothing and think about nothing but our own oft-rehearsed lines.

John Gottman's research on marriage has made an intriguing discovery that is related to the challenges of parenting. When couples are angry and insult each other, they may think they are being clever and creative. But Gottman's research shows that angry couples follow a tired, familiar path. He even describes the four stages in the conflict process.[28] In contrast, when couples are happy, it is impossible to predict what they will do next.

The keen irony is that meanness is not remotely creative. It is trite and tiresome. Conflict is the theme and it is dreary, predictable stuff.

In contrast, when we listen to the better angels of our nature, we are genuinely creative. We are original, imaginative, inventive, and ingenious! We enjoy our children and our lives.

So, rather than play the age-old, shrewish role of villain, we can step out of our part and take a seat in the audience. From that vantage point we may be able to see that our day's stress is speaking more loudly than any discernment about the child's motives and needs. We may be able to see a struggling and imperfect child confronted by a tired, irritated, and imperfect parent. If we can extract ourselves from the thoughts and emotions, we may be able to write a new—and more creative—part for us to play.

I remember sitting with Shirley W., the principal at a school for children with disabilities. When a class bell rang and two boys came to her door, she excused herself from our conversation. One boy told her about the things he had accomplished. She warmly congratulated him. The second boy asked, "What about me?" She reflected. Then she exploded, "I heard what you did to the substitute teacher today." She grabbed the little boy and pulled him close. "You're too good a person to act that way! If you ever do that again, I will hug you senseless."

I fought back tears. Shirley had risen above the usual rant and threats. She chose to step out of the familiar part. She chose instead to send a clear message of affection—with limits.

Once we have applied life-affirming creativity to re-writing our parenting parts, we may re-enter the play. Maybe we decide that we will confront the Big Issue later—but right now, let's hug. Or let's cook dinner. Or let's go buy a pizza. You just never know what you will come up with when joy is your playwright.

Reflection

Think of a time when you have removed yourself from the automatic and unhelpful responses and have let goodness fill your heart. How did it feel? What helped you get there? How can you get there again? How can you make that experience more common for you?

Applying this Strategy

☐ I don't think this will work for me.

☐ This is something I am already good at and use regularly to good effect.

☐ This is something I haven't tried but would like to try.

    Next time [insert your parenting dilemma] happens, I'm going to try [insert your personal solution that applies this strategy].

    Write a plan.

Visualize yourself doing it.

☐ This is something I have tried but need to practice.

Next time [insert your parenting dilemma] happens, I'm going to try [insert your personal solution that applies this strategy].

Write a plan.

Visualize yourself doing it.

Notes on progress: _____

_____

_____

_____

_____

20.

Go Walking

Research has shown that mild exercise—such as walking—may be the most reliable way to lift our moods.

Religious leader David McKay suggested walking as a solution for heated tempers between a man and his wife: "When you get into a discussion, only one get angry at a time. . . . You go outside and walk around the block, and then when you get back home, throw your hat in the door. If it comes back out again, walk around the block another time."[29]

The same general principle applies in relationships with our children. When we are angry, we would do well to take a walk. As George Jean Nathan observed, "No man can think clearly when his fists are clenched." Taking a walk can clear our heads and unclench our mental fists.

The walk is likely to be helpful if we use the time to enjoy the natural world. The time is likely to be unproductive if we mentally heap hot coals upon our children's heads.

So, when we're feeling angry or irritable, we might take a walk. We can enjoy nature. We might even reflect on the mistakes *we* made that irritated *our* parents. There are also times when we might take the offending child with us—not to lecture or threaten—but to relax. As our focus turns from our irritation to our blessings, we are likely to have a more helpful perspective.

Our son, Andy, has always been very enthusiastic. That scared me many times when Andy was a new driver. So, time and again, I asked him to slow down, be careful, take driving seriously. His glib "Sure, Dad" did not bring me much comfort.

One night Andy found me in the kitchen and somberly announced, "We need to talk." My heart sank. We went to his room. He told me about driving around with his friends, acting silly, weaving between lanes, and accidentally cutting off a van. The driver was angry and followed him and took down his license number. Andy was expecting a squad of armed police to surround our house any minute.

I was relieved that nothing worse had happened. But I was also angry that Andy had been careless. I was angry that he had not taken my many warnings seriously. So I did what parents are trained to do. I preached. "Andy, what is wrong with you? Why can't you ever learn? How many times do I have to tell you?" I went on quite a while. I finally noticed that I was making myself sick.

So I stopped. I asked if I might start over again—if we might walk together along a different lane. Andy wasn't sure if that was a good idea, but he consented.

I told him about the time when I was a high school senior and I was our driving around with my early-teen cousins and they spotted a couple in love in the truck behind us. We started making fun of them. My cousins played like they were in love. I played with the blinkers. After a while it became clear that the fellow behind us did not think our horseplay was funny. So I turned off the highway.

I was dismayed to find that he followed us. I was dismayed to find that I was on a dead-end road. I was dismayed to find that when I stopped at the end of the road he parked right behind us. I was really dismayed to discover when he got out of his truck that he was wearing a university football jacket.

But I thought I would be cool. Just sit there and play like he wasn't there. He came to the side window and made me an offer: "Would you like me to break this window and drag you through it or would you like to step out for me to beat you?"

Two inviting options. I chose to step out. And he shared some thoughts and feelings with me that I still remember.

When I finished telling the story to Andy, I paused. "Andy, sometimes we learn lessons the hard way. But it is so important that we learn them." Long silence.

Finally, Andy said, "Thanks, dad."

"You're welcome, son. I love you."

When I was yelling and lecturing, any useful information was lost in the fury and anger.

When I walked side by side with Andy, we both grew.

Reflection

Think of a time when you have taken a walk to calm yourself. How did it feel? What helped you get there? How can you get there again? How can you make that experience more common for you?

Applying this Strategy

☐ I don't think this will work for me.
☐ This is something I am already good at and use regularly to good effect.
☐ This is something I haven't tried but would like to try.

> Next time [insert your parenting dilemma] happens, I'm going to try [insert your personal solution that applies this strategy].

>> Write a plan.

Visualize yourself doing it.

☐ This is something I have tried but need to practice.

Next time [insert your parenting dilemma] happens,
I'm going to try [insert your personal solution that
applies this strategy].

Write a plan.

Visualize yourself doing it.

Notes on progress: _____

_____

_____

_____

_____

21.

Think Graciously

I once read a story about an older woman who went to the grocery store and bought just a few items almost every day. The clerks wondered about this. Why didn't she buy groceries for a week? Why did she come in every day and buy just a few items? They couldn't figure out the answer, so one of the clerks determined to ask the woman. The next day, when the lady was ready to check out, the clerk asked, "Ma'am, why is it that you shop every day and buy just a few items?" The woman sighed, "I'm a widow. I live with my nephew—and I hate his guts. When I die, I don't intend to leave him any groceries!"

That is a good example of small-minded thinking. We keep score and we make sure that we don't bless anyone we don't like. Notice that this mind-set puts us in a role for which we humans are ill-suited. We decide each person's merit and we decide his or her reward.

We humans do a very poor job of playing God.

Some of us have a lot of faith in the educational value of suffering. We assume that making children suffer will help them learn. In my view, that is dangerous thinking.

Bertrand Russell observed that "the reformative effect of punishment is a belief that dies hard, chiefly, I think, because [punishment] is so satisfying to our sadistic impulses."[30]

Sadism is not the basis of good parenting. We want our children to learn the lessons of life. And the message of experience and research is clear: People learn best when they feel loved.

I enjoy the story of a sweet six-year-old girl named Marcie who was confined to the hospital for a serious lung disorder. During her hospital stay, one of her baby teeth fell out. She put it under the pillow hoping that the tooth fairy could find her at the hospital. The night nurse was assigned to take the tooth and slip a dollar bill under her pillow. Because she loved little Marcie so much, she determined to put two dollars under her pillow when she took the tooth.

But it wasn't easy to find the chance to get the tooth. In the course of the evening there were various therapists, aides, and nurses. But finally she found the right moment and slipped the money under the pillow.

The next morning the head nurse asked how it went. The nurse observed that it had been a busy evening but she had done her job. The head nurse replied: "It must have been busy. This morning there was $12 under her pillow!"

That is graciousness! While I'm not sure that $12 is a reasonable price for a baby tooth, I applaud the spirit of love and appreciation that motivated the generosity.

Reflection

Think of a time when you have thought about a child graciously—wanting to bless, teach, and encourage him or her. How did it feel? What helped you get there? How can you get there again? How can you make that experience more common for you?

Applying this Strategy

☐ I don't think this will work for me.
☐ This is something I am already good at and use regularly to good effect.
☐ This is something I haven't tried but would like to try.
　　Next time [insert your parenting dilemma] happens,

I'm going to try [insert your personal solution that applies this strategy].

> Write a plan.
>
> Visualize yourself doing it.

☐ This is something I have tried but need to practice.

> Next time [insert your parenting dilemma] happens, I'm going to try [insert your personal solution that applies this strategy].

> > Write a plan.
> >
> > Visualize yourself doing it.

Notes on progress: _____

_____

_____

_____

_____

22.

Invite a Debate

A dear friend called me very agitated one day and asked to see me. We met. She told me that she had discovered that her husband had been stealing from his employer. She was furious. She intended to leave him.

We talked. We discussed learning and weaknesses and patience. After about an hour she was resolved to return to her marriage and try to help her husband. As we parted, I asked her, "Why did you come to me when you knew I would not encourage you to divorce?" She replied immediately, "That is why I came to you! I needed someone who could help me find a way to stay. I knew you would do that."

I applaud her integrity. Even though she wanted to leave a challenging relationship, she sought counsel that would help her stay.

We can do the same. When we are determined to act in ways that are lower than our highest standards, we can seek counsel from those we know will pull us up to our full stature. Who do you know whose love of goodness is so great that they will challenge your less noble actions?

In an ideal family, our spouses do this for us often. When the raging fire in our souls is pushing us to act harshly, a faithful spouse can invite us to set aside the rage in favor of reason. In fact, we may work with our spouse at peaceful times to develop a signal for just such emergencies.

When Nancy sees my temperature rise above the rational range, she might invite, "I know you've been wanting to mow the lawn out back. Why don't you do that and then we can talk about the children later this evening."

In some cases we may be able to find that nobler voice in our own souls.

We may be able to challenge our own less-than-noble impulses.

My wise father used to say that many decisions are difficult mainly because we are trying to justify an action that is less than our highest standard. Another way to identify a bad decision is to notice when we are trying way too hard to convince ourselves.

The way Shakespeare described this condition is: "The lady doth protest too much, methinks."[31] Rather than strut and moralize to justify thoughts and actions that we know to be less than they ought, we can change. And when we need help to do it, we can invite those who are friends to goodness to challenge us.

Reflection

Think of a time when you have invited a debate—when you have challenged your less noble thoughts with input from a spouse, friends, or your own better nature—in order to avoid an angry attack. How did it feel? What helped you get there? How can you get there again? How can you make that experience more common for you?

Applying this Strategy

☐ I don't think this will work for me.

☐ This is something I am already good at and use regularly to good effect.

☐ This is something I haven't tried but would like to try.

Next time [insert your parenting dilemma] happens, I'm going to try [insert your personal solution that applies this strategy].

Write a plan.

Visualize yourself doing it.

☐ This is something I have tried but need to practice.

Next time [insert your parenting dilemma] happens,

I'm going to try [insert your personal solution that applies this strategy].

Write a plan.

Visualize yourself doing it.

Notes on progress: _____

_____

_____

_____

_____

23.

Feed Your Own Soul

"Out of the abundance of the heart, the mouth speaketh."[32] A parched, arid heart cannot sustain life or goodness.

There are many ways to feed our spirits. But there is a trick to doing it right. Many of us try to feed our souls in the way that works for this person or that. Or we try to do the things we have heard are guaranteed soul-builders. But, when we tramp along the road of obligation as if we were on a death march, our souls do not get fed. In other words, each of us must find the unique way that best feeds us.

Meditation may work for your neighbor but not for you. Reading may work for you while jogging does not. Home improvements projects are restorative for one person and drudgery for another.

In spite of this diversity in ways of finding renewal, the best research on happiness[33] suggests three general ways to increase our well-being. First, we can savor or appreciate the blessings in our lives. Trite but true, happiness depends less on getting what we want than on enjoying what we have. In more scientific terms:

> Trying to find happiness by striving to obtain more possessions in the future may backfire. Indeed, a wealth of evidence indicated that the single-minded goal of achieving happiness through efforts to attain more material goods is self-defeating.[34]

That pop psychologist Pollyanna was wiser than many realize: The glad game is good for our hearts and our happiness. A whole new field of psychology is growing around the idea of savoring life experience.

The second way we can increase our happiness is by figuring out what our talents are and designing our lives so we can use them regularly. This is related to flow which is psychology's name for the state when we get so involved with a challenging task that we lose track of time. Just like the memorable quote by Eric Liddell from Chariots of Fire: "I believe God made me for a purpose, but he also made me fast. And when I run I feel His pleasure."

Most of us will never run as Liddell did. But we might find profound satisfaction in engineering a bridge, ordering a household, teaching school, or framing houses. That is the key to a good life.

The third way to increase happiness is by serving. When we dedicate some part of our lives and energies to making others' lives better, our own lives get better.

Those are the three processes for growing our happiness. So we cultivate a grateful heart, we design our lives to use our talents, and we find ways to make the world a better place. Those are all effective ways to feed our spirit.

Reflection

Think of a time when you have fed your spirit—when you have done things that brought you joy, growth, and satisfaction. How did it feel? What helped you get there? How can you get there again? How can you make that experience more common for you?

Applying this Strategy

- [ ] I don't think this will work for me.
- [ ] This is something I am already good at and use regularly to good effect.

☐ This is something I haven't tried but would like to try.

    Next time [insert your parenting dilemma] happens, I'm going to try [insert your personal solution that applies this strategy].

        Write a plan.

        Visualize yourself doing it.

☐ This is something I have tried but need to practice.

    Next time [insert your parenting dilemma] happens, I'm going to try [insert your personal solution that applies this strategy].

        Write a plan.

        Visualize yourself doing it.

Notes on progress: _____

_____

_____

_____

_____

24.

Put It into Perspective

Just as I was finishing graduate school, Nancy and I bought an almost-new car. It was quite a contrast with our old station wagon with fake wood siding that was peeling off. Our children felt that the days of their humiliation might finally be over.

I remember the first time I drove the car off the lot after signing the papers. As I sat in the driver's seat enjoying the many things that worked properly, I noticed a small dent in the hood. Perhaps a mechanic had bent over the car and dented the hood with a tire gauge in his shirt pocket. It was a small dent. But for several months it was the only thing I saw when I looked at the car. I hardly noticed the shiny paint, the uncracked upholstery, or the hardy engine. I only saw the dent.

Most of us do the same thing in family life. We notice the little thing that isn't quite right. Sometimes it is the only thing we notice.

Our son Andy has always been creative. As he got older he got more and more artistic. He has always been a kind, generous, and respectful boy. But, when he was a teenager, his creativity was more evident in his room than was his respect for the family rule about keeping his room clean.

We would remind him, but the creative projects would still accumulate. We would "consequence" him and leave his unhampered laundry unwashed. But he just didn't worry about tidiness the way his perfectionistic dad did.

We had two choices. We could increase the volume on the demand. Or we could let it go. We chose to let it go. We did not want to torch a relationship with our son for the sake of a little tidiness. (We did reserve the right to close his door when the disarray bothered us. And, once in a while, we asked if he would humor us by tidying things. He did so gladly.)

Many of the power struggles between parents and children are about matters of taste and preference. A mother may not like her daughter wearing T-shirts to school. It may suggest disrespect and rebellion to the mom. To the daughter it is merely a matter of personal expression.

If we over-interpret children's behavior as signifying rebellion, we are likely to over-react, over-control, and create rebellion. In matters of principle, we should be firm. In matters of preference, we should be tolerant.

In contrast, if a child is wanting to buy a prom dress that is clearly suggestive or immodest, we can empathize with her desire while setting a firm limit: "I can see why you like the dress. The fabric is elegant. But we don't buy gowns that expose that much of your body. Have you seen others that you like or do we need to keep looking?"

We can deliver a firm message without ever becoming disagreeable. When our daughter cries in desperation, "Mom! It's not that bad. It is exactly the dress I want. And Becky has one just like it. Don't be such a prude!" We can keep our balance. "Wow. You really like that dress! And I can see why. Since it does not meet our standard, we can look at some other store or we might look online. Which sounds good to you?"

If we believe that we must convince our children that we are right and if we expect them to appreciate our principles and logic in every moment, we will be disappointed. Good parenting requires us to set some limits that children will dislike. Sometimes good children will be very angry with their wise parents. But we can always be pleasant.

At the same time we recognize that a lot of little choices should be left to them. Most clothing decisions and room décor should be allowed to the child's preference.

Reflection: Think of a time when you have put children's actions in perspective—overlooking little mistakes and allowing them to follow their preferences. How did it feel? What helped you get there? How can you get there again? How can you make that experience more common for you?

Applying this Strategy

☐ I don't think this will work for me.

☐ This is something I am already good at and use regularly to good effect.

☐ This is something I haven't tried but would like to try.

> Next time [insert your parenting dilemma] happens, I'm going to try [insert your personal solution that applies this strategy].
>
> > Write a plan.
> >
> > Visualize yourself doing it.

☐ This is something I have tried but need to practice.

> Next time [insert your parenting dilemma] happens, I'm going to try [insert your personal solution that applies this strategy].
>
> > Write a plan.
> >
> > Visualize yourself doing it.

Notes on progress: _____

_____

_____

_____

_____

25.

Invite Each Child to be Part of a Solution

Children tend to fight and quarrel with each other. As we resist the temptation to fight and quarrel with them, we can teach them better ways. Rather than use our greater authority and size, we can teach the use of civilized processes for solving problems.

In my youth, I often picked fights with my brother Alan, who is a good-hearted, compassionate, good-natured guy. I myself have never had any real preference for unkindness or violence. But we still teased each other endlessly. I resolved disputes by locking Alan in a hall closet as long as I was bigger than he. As we moved into adolescence and Alan became sturdier than I was, I turned to goading and tormenting him verbally.

Mom and Dad tried everything they could think of to help us settle differences and to encourage peace. On one occasion after I had been tormenting Alan, and when all efforts at negotiation and calm persuasion had failed, Dad suggested we wrestle. Well, Alan whipped me, which, incidentally, did not bring peace and understanding to our relationship; my determination to conquer only increased. On another occasion Mom and Dad suggested that we settle our differences through a foot race. I outdistanced Alan. I am certain that his bond with me was not strengthened by being beaten in a foot race.

These methods of resolving differences did not bring peace and understanding—though they may have marginally increased our physical fitness. In fact, one strategy for dealing with bickering might be to direct children's anger toward physical contests and hope that maturity would set in to quell the rivalries. Such a decades-long process may have some advantages, yet it cannot teach children the skills of peacemaking.

I remember an occasion when Alan and I had been arguing over some small difference. Dad, a peace-loving man if ever there was one, was weary of the contention. He turned both of us to face him and invited each of us to tell our side of the story. Alan, through tears, told of my picking on him and rude treatment of him. When it was my turn, I calmly and sensibly told of Alan's misdeeds and carefully wove psychological explanation into the tale. As I told my story I warmed to the challenge and embellished the story with plausible though invented details. I knew that my Father was a very rational man. Alan was more likely to be judged in error by Dad. The only thing that process revealed was that I had a greater talent for creative storytelling than Alan. Or, to be fair, I was better at lying than Alan who is, to this day, a very fine storyteller.

There were times when Mom held the warring factions to an accounting. Mother, always sensitive to the underdog and emotional suffering, was more likely to feel compassion for Alan and zero in on my error.

The irony with investigating warring children's stories is that every party in a war contributes something to the misunderstanding. While one party may contribute far more than another, it is impossible for any of us mortals to weigh guilt objectively and dispassionately. We all have biases.

My battles with Alan and the accounting before our parents underscore what may be the first law of human dynamics: When someone tries to take something away from us, we cling to it more tenaciously. If Dad or Mom tried to convince me that I was wrong, I would renew my data collecting and analyzing to prove I was right. I would also add passion and indignation.

Given that the human tendency to see ourselves as right is almost universal, what's a parent to do? How can we move people from the natural tendency to stake out a territory and defend it at all costs? How can we keep people from exaggerating their differences? How can we teach cooperation and harmony? How can we hope to establish peace in our families?

I have an idea. Imagine that Dad had very attentively listened to the two separate dramas as if they did not have to be woven into one story. He could listen for each person's personal reality. He might have said to Alan, "Son, it sounds as if you are tired of being pushed around. It sounds like you would like to be able to play in your bedroom without your brother telling you to get lost. Is that right?" Alan, through words and gestures, will tell Dad whether he has captured the emotional essence of his experience.

Then Dad might turn to me. "Wally, it sounds as if you would like to be able to work on your projects without being interrupted. You would like your brother not to bother you when you are in the middle of something. Is that right?" As Dad attempts to understand each of our perspectives, he is inviting our cooperation and trust.

When each of us feels understood, we are prepared to offer compassion. We are ready to look for solutions. "I wonder if you boys have any ideas how you can help each other." In such a setting I might have volunteered, "Well, I could be nicer to Alan. And I could let him know when I really need him to be quiet."

At Dad's invitation Alan might have volunteered to be quieter when he could see that I was concentrating. He might also have volunteered to play outside when I was working on some projects.

When people are looking for solutions rather than problems, wonderful things can happen. When their better natures have been invoked, people may choose to offer kindness and sacrifice for the common good.

By the way, I cannot imagine that anyone on the face of the earth had better parents than Alan and I had. But no one ever taught our folks how to draw solutions out of us kids. As we apply peacemaking skills to our children's squabbles, we assure both present and future peace.

Reflection

Think of a time when you have invited your children to be part of the solution in their disagreements with their siblings. How did it feel? What helped you get there? How can you get there again? How can you make that experience more common for you?

Applying this Strategy

☐ I don't think this will work for me.

☐ This is something I am already good at and use regularly to good effect.

☐ This is something I haven't tried but would like to try.

> Next time [insert your parenting dilemma] happens, I'm going to try [insert your personal solution that applies this strategy].
>
> > Write a plan.
> >
> > Visualize yourself doing it.

☐ This is something I have tried but need to practice.

> Next time [insert your parenting dilemma] happens, I'm going to try [insert your personal solution that applies this strategy].
>
> > Write a plan.
> >
> > Visualize yourself doing it.

Notes on progress: _____

_____

_____

_____

_____

26.

Choose to See the Good

I remember a story about a Little League coach who had players who just didn't get baseball. They rarely hit the ball and couldn't seem to remember which way to run the bases. Naturally, they didn't win many games. In fact, they lost every game of the season.

Then came the last game of the season. In the last inning of that last game, the coach's team was only down by one run. As fate would have it, the next person up to bat was a little boy who had never hit the ball or caught it in the entire season. Since there were two outs against the team already, the team was ready to bag the bats and balls ending the season without a single win.

But somehow that little boy connected with the pitch. After some pause for amazement, he made his way to first base. At this point the guys realized that the next batter was their best. Hopes rose. The team might end the season with a win!

The ball was pitched. The slugger hit it squarely toward right field! With a little coaching, the feckless boy on first headed toward second base. But he hadn't gone very far before he saw the ball coming toward him. He had never been in this situation. He wasn't sure what to do.

So he caught the ball making the final out. The coach's team lost the game and the season.

The coach must have been shocked. He thought for a moment and then turned to his stunned team. "Cheer for that boy! He has never before hit the ball or caught it and he just did both in the same inning!"

The boy's parents later thanked the coach. That little boy had never even been played in a game before that season. Now he was a local hero. That coach saw good where others might have seen failure. He saw progress.

Research[35] shows a clear way of discouraging ourselves and others. When anyone makes a mistake, we can make it personal, permanent, and pervasive (note the 3 Ps). To the child who forgets to feed the dog, the discouraging statement might be: "How could you be so careless?! What's wrong with you?" (personal); "It seems like you never remember anything!" (permanent); "You forget your homework, you forget to take your lunch to school. You forget your chores." (pervasive); "I think you would forget your head if it weren't screwed on" (pervasive).

While the parent may intend to motivate more reliable remembering, the child will almost surely experience discouragement. In contrast, a parent might choose to see the good. "You usually remember to feed the dog. You must have a lot on your mind."

By making the problem situational, temporary, and limited, the child is more likely to see it as solvable. In fact, a parent might ask, "What could you do to help yourself remember to feed the dog? Would it help to put a reminder on your closet door?"

Of course choosing to see the good is not limited to seeing good in bad situations. We should notice and appreciate the many small ways children try to be helpful. "Thank you for helping your brother." "Thank you for helping me clear the table." "Thank you for that big hug. You made my day!"

Reflection

Think of a time when you have chosen to see the good in a child—when you could have ignored the behavior or could have been negative but instead chose to see the good. How did it feel? What helped you get there?

How can you get there again? How can you make that experience more common for you?

Applying this Strategy

☐ I don't think this will work for me.

☐ This is something I am already good at and use regularly to good effect.

☐ This is something I haven't tried but would like to try.

    Next time [insert your parenting dilemma] happens, I'm going to try [insert your personal solution that applies this strategy].

        Write a plan.

        Visualize yourself doing it.

☐ This is something I have tried but need to practice.

    Next time [insert your parenting dilemma] happens, I'm going to try [insert your personal solution that applies this strategy].

        Write a plan.

        Visualize yourself doing it.

Notes on progress: _____

_____

_____

_____

_____

27.

Invite the Child to Talk You Out of It

As children get older they should be more and more involved in guiding their own lives. There may be times when we are inclined to be angry with a child or impose a stern penalty, but we are not sure what will help them. Maybe we could ask them. We can invite children to tell us what would help them remember their chores, get ready for school, or be helpful with a sibling.

When we are inclined to impose a stiff penalty designed more by anger than reason, we can instead invite the child to help us find the right consequence. "After what you said to your sister, I'm tempted to remove all your privileges for decades. I'm really upset. I need you to tell me what would help you take this seriously."

The children usually know better than we do the things that will help the messages sink in for them.

Reflection

Think of a time when you have let a child help you design the consequence for his or her misdeeds. How did it feel? What helped you get there? How can you get there again? How can you make that experience more common for you?

Applying this Strategy

- [ ] I don't think this will work for me.
- [ ] This is something I am already good at and use regularly to good effect.
- [ ] This is something I haven't tried but would like to try.

Next time [insert your parenting dilemma] happens,
I'm going to try [insert your personal solution that
applies this strategy].

    Write a plan.

    Visualize yourself doing it.

☐ This is something I have tried but need to practice.

Next time [insert your parenting dilemma] happens,
I'm going to try [insert your personal solution that
applies this strategy].

    Write a plan.

    Visualize yourself doing it.

Notes on progress: _____

_____

_____

_____

_____

28.

Plan for Children's Misdeeds and Needs

Arthur Bowler wrote about a minister and his cherished hymnal. One day the minister's two-year-old son got a hold of the book and applied a pen to making scribbles all over the first page. When his father walked into the room, the little boy cowered. The father, a man who cherished his books, walked to the boy, picked up the hymnal, studied it carefully, and sat down without a word. The little boy awaited his punishment. But rather than punish or scold, the father took the pen from the boy's hand and wrote alongside the scribbles, "John's word 1959, age two."

When we let love rule in our hearts, our reactions are very different from those when anger rules. This father chose to see the book enriched and sanctified by the scribbles of his cherished boy.

Van Wyck Brooks has written, "How delightful is the company of generous people, who overlook trifles and keep their minds instinctively fixed on whatever is good and positive in the world about them. People of small caliber are always carping. They are bent on showing their own superiority, their knowledge or prowess or good breeding. But magnanimous people have no vanity, they have no jealousy, and they feed on the true and the solid wherever they find it. And, what is more, they find it everywhere."[36]

Unfortunately it is quite natural for us to expect adult behavior from children. It is natural to wish they did not inconvenience our very important adult lives.

William Faulkner apparently knew how to honor his relationship with his little girl. The great author made an informal presentation at the University of Mississippi. The student assigned to guide him had been anxious about interacting with a man of genius and fame but found that he was completely approachable and down-to-earth.

Faulkner had spent more than two hours with the students and faculty when his guide noticed him checking his watch. The guide wondered if he had an important commitment or had grown impatient with the students. She asked him if he needed to leave. He replied, "Well, it's just that I promised my daughter Jill that I'd help her shell corn for the chickens and I don't want to disappoint her."

The noblest souls are those who honor their commitment to love and cherish their children—in spite of their childishness.

Reflection

Think of a time when you have planned for children's misdeeds and demands—when you have managed graciousness in the face of frustration. How did it feel? What helped you get there? How can you get there again? How can you make that experience more common for you?

Applying this Strategy

☐ I don't think this will work for me.

☐ This is something I am already good at and use regularly to good effect.

☐ This is something I haven't tried but would like to try.

  Next time [insert your parenting dilemma] happens, I'm going to try [insert your personal solution that applies this strategy].

   Write a plan.

   Visualize yourself doing it.

☐ This is something I have tried but need to practice.

  Next time [insert your parenting dilemma] happens, I'm going to try [insert your personal solution that

applies this strategy].

Write a plan.

Visualize yourself doing it.

Notes on progress: _____

_____

_____

_____

_____

29.

Rewrite the Story

A mother caught me after a parenting workshop seeking advice. She began, "Last night while my daughter was studying, I cooked dinner for her. It's something she loves. When I took it to her, she turned up her nose at it. I was indignant. I chewed her out and told her she was grounded for a week for acting that way." The mother paused before proceeding, "The punishment seems extreme. But I don't want to go back on my word. What should I do?" Both mother and daughter felt awful about the confrontation. And both were trapped in their resentment.

The mother wisely recognized that making threats and failing to enforce them sends mixed messages to children. Yet, as parents, we don't need to be trapped by past mistakes. There is another option. I recommended that they work together to rewrite the story:

"This afternoon when your daughter gets home from school, ask her if you can take some time to visit. When you are comfortably seated, tell her that you were upset last night. You felt that your daughter was not very appreciative. Then, admitting your regret, you can acknowledge that your reaction was not one you feel good about. You took her lack of appreciation personally and reacted emotionally. Ask her if you could both erase last night's unpleasantness and start over again. Tell her that you love her more than life itself and you never want a small misunderstanding to become a big barrier between you."

The mother looked very relieved by the suggestion. She knew what would happen after the new beginning to the old story. She knew that her daughter would grab her mother and apologize. She knew that they would once again be joined in love. Grounding was superfluous.

Some time in the future the daughter will again be unappreciative. It is inevitable. But Mom has scripted a better reaction. She might say, "Ouch! I had hoped to delight you with one of your favorite meals. I'm disappointed that you're not pleased." When the daughter knows her mother's intentions, she is likely to react more gently. It is also possible that, in the future, the mother would ask the daughter if she would like her to make a snack for her before investing the effort.

Good parenting is nothing more than the continuing process of learning to be wiser and better as we help our children become strong and compassionate humans.

Reflection

Think of a time when you have rewritten a sad story—when you have gone back to repair an unhelpful reaction. How did it feel? What helped you get there? How can you get there again? How can you make that experience more common for you?

Applying this Strategy

☐ I don't think this will work for me.

☐ This is something I am already good at and use regularly to good effect.

☐ This is something I haven't tried but would like to try.

    Next time [insert your parenting dilemma] happens, I'm going to try [insert your personal solution that applies this strategy].

        Write a plan.

        Visualize yourself doing it.

☐ This is something I have tried but need to practice.

    Next time [insert your parenting dilemma] happens, I'm going to try [insert your personal solution that applies this strategy].

Write a plan.
Visualize yourself doing it.

Notes on progress: _____

_____

_____

_____

_____

30.

Imagine Yourself as Aunt Mary

Aunt Mary and Uncle Grant lived in a small town in southern Utah. Every summer they invited us to come visit them. As an adult I have wondered why they invited us; we added to their burdens. Yet, they seemed to genuinely enjoy us. And they tolerated our antics without visible chagrin. When I crashed his motor scooter with no injury to me but no benefit for the scooter, Uncle Grant merely laughed. When Alan and I narrowly avoided burning down all of southern Utah, Aunt Mary simply turned on the sprinklers to cool us off as we dragged ourselves back to her house.

There is something magical about a person who seems to genuinely enjoy you in spite of your foibles and misdeeds. I'm grateful for Aunt Mary and Uncle Grant.

Maybe you know someone who has always seen the best in you. Maybe your life has been blessed by that person's generosity. Think back to the sweet blessing of that heavenly gift. Savor it. Relive specific episodes.

Now, are we ready to be Aunt Marys for our children? Are we ready to look beyond their goofiness and see their spunk? Are we willing to be inconvenienced by the demands of parenting? Are we willing to bring surprise and joy to our relationship?

When we fill our souls with remembered goodness, we are better prepared to offer grace to those we love. We can offer a special picnic, a trip to the zoo, an outing in the backyard. And we can savor every moment.

Reflection

Think of a time when you have been an Aunt Mary for one of your children. How did it feel? What helped you get there? How can you get there again? How can you make that experience more common for you?

Applying this Strategy

☐ I don't think this will work for me.

☐ This is something I am already good at and use regularly to good effect.

☐ This is something I haven't tried but would like to try.

    Next time [insert your parenting dilemma] happens, I'm going to try [insert your personal solution that applies this strategy].

        Write a plan.

        Visualize yourself doing it.

☐ This is something I have tried but need to practice.

    Next time [insert your parenting dilemma] happens, I'm going to try [insert your personal solution that applies this strategy].

        Write a plan.

        Visualize yourself doing it.

Notes on progress: _____

_____

_____

_____

_____

31.

Get Help

When we're overwhelmed, overloaded, and over-stressed, our children are likely to get a brittle, demanding parent. We may not realize how different we seem to our children. In fact, our pain can make us oblivious to their struggles and feelings.

Some dear friends wrote to us from a distant city asking for advice in helping their son, the older of their two boys. Once in a while he seemed to go crazy, running around the house and jumping on the furniture in defiance of family rules. Mom and Dad emailed me, asking what they could do.

I wrote back the standard advice about noticing the stress in the child's life, being sure he has loving time with mom and dad, and giving him many chances to use his energy and talents. When I didn't hear back from them for some time, I hoped things were going better.

Then we got another email asking for a chance to talk by phone. "We're so frustrated we fear that we will hurt our little boy." We set a time to talk.

At the appointed time, they called us. For more than an hour we talked about the boy's stresses, his loving opportunities with parents, and ways to use his energy. But we didn't find the answer to the crazy episodes.

In desperation, I asked the mom, "Is there anything different from the usual in *your* life at the time of these episodes?"

Mom heaved a sigh. "Every once in a while I am up all night with the baby when he is sick. When morning comes, I am exhausted. Our problems almost always occur when I am sitting nursing the baby after being up all night."

I asked the logical follow-up question: "Is your boy pretty sensitive to your moods?"

Her immediate response: "He's very sensitive! He notices anytime anything is bothering me."

We had our answer. Every once in a while, the "terrorist" boy would get up and find that his normally-cheerful, loving mother was distant and gloomy. He would feel worried, anxious, insecure. His behavior was his way of saying, "Mom, where are you? I need you! Please play with me! Please talk to me! Please be my mommy!" The little troublemaker was really just an anxious child who wanted his mama back.

Though it helps to understand the problem, there is no easy solution for it. Understanding the boy's anxiety, Mom might explain her exhaustion to him: "Son, I was up most of the night with the baby last night. I am very tired. I am sorry that I don't have the energy to laugh and play with you right now."

She might also call a friend and ask if the son can play at their house while she takes a nap. Dad might take some time from work to care for the boys while his wife rests. They might call on a grandparent or a babysitter.

There are times when every parent needs a helping hand. That help may come from spouse, extended family, friend, or professional. When we are overloaded, we should get help.

Reflection

Think of a time when you have been overloaded and have gotten help. How did it feel to draw in the needed resources? What helped you get there? How can you get there again when appropriate?

Applying this Strategy

☐ I don't think this will work for me.

☐ This is something I am already good at and use regularly to good effect.

☐ This is something I haven't tried but would like to try.

Next time [insert your parenting dilemma] happens, I'm going to try [insert your personal solution that applies this strategy].

Write a plan.

Visualize yourself doing it.

☐ This is something I have tried but need to practice.

Next time [insert your parenting dilemma] happens, I'm going to try [insert your personal solution that applies this strategy].

Write a plan.

Visualize yourself doing it.

Notes on progress: _____

_____

_____

_____

_____

32.

Haul Off the Trash and Open the Windows

> Housing officials in Spokane, Wash., Tuesday gave
> cleanup deadlines to Kathleen Henry, whose house is so
> filthy it has sickened garbage workers. The city plans to
> demolish the home if she misses the deadlines. Officials
> say there are animal feces on floors and garbage stacked
> to the ceilings. Two trash collectors became ill March 17,
> so firefighters with respirators finished the job.[37]

It is hard to imagine a house so filled with trash! Imagine the odor! Imagine the challenge of navigating between piles of garbage! Imagine sitting for a meal in the midst of the stench! Such a pile of trash would take over family life and intrude on every activity.

The same may be true when we let emotional, social, and spiritual debris accumulate in our lives. In one corner of our hearts is resentment for people who have neglected us. In the middle of the floor is hostility for family members who have cheated us, judged us, and hurt us. Hanging over our happiness is a haze of sullenness for children who disappoint us. The piles of stinking garbage can pile up and make it impossible to conduct normal life without tripping on the piles or choking on the foul odor. Such a mess makes the prospect of love very remote.

Human nature is perverse. Sometimes the only way we know to be "happy" is by being unhappy. We cling to resentment, hostility, and sullenness. Thomas Clayton Wolfe put it pointedly: "Poor, dismal, ugly, sterile, shabby little man . . . with your scrabble of harsh oaths . . . Joy, glory, and magnificence were here for you . . . but you scrabbled along . . . rattling a few stale words . . . and would have none of them."[38]

How do we deal with the piles of stinking garbage that accumulate in our family life? We can study the garbage and its sources. We can learn to live with it. We can wallow in it.

Or we can bundle it up, haul it to the curbside, and be done with it. We can throw open the windows to fresh air and sunshine. We can part with sodden trash and replace it with fresh, life-sustaining provisions.

Resentment is remedied with forgiveness. Hostility is healed by choosing to love. Disappointment is cured by finding positive purpose in our lives.

Sometimes the enemy of family closeness is more subtle than accumulations of trash. Our relationships may be stale rather than stinking. We fail to enjoy close relationships because we simply fail to open the windows to them. We neglect the people who can mean the most to us.

I remember when Andy was small, maybe three or four years old. He used to like to sleep in odd places such as the linen closet or an empty bathtub. One night he asked if he could sleep on the floor in his sister's room. After consulting with Emily, it was agreed that he would spread his sleeping bag on the floor in front of her old dresser. So we arranged his bedding on the floor and he went to sleep. But in the wee hours of the morning, I was awakened from a sound sleep by a muffled cry.

Somehow I knew instinctively what had happened. I knew that the old dresser with a bad leg had somehow had the supporting can of paint knocked out from under it and that the dresser had fallen over on our sleeping son. I found myself launched from my bed and unbidden words escaping from the deepest part of my soul: *"No! Not my Andy!"* I ran to the bedroom and found the heavy dresser covering my son. I immediately pulled it off him and dragged it into the hall. Then I comforted Andy. Fortunately he was not badly hurt.

After some loving, he returned to sleep. (I promptly found a saw and cut off the other three legs to match the broken one so that the dresser would never fall over again on a beloved child.)

That experience with Andy helped me remember that Andy, Emily, and Sara mean more to me than life itself. So I work to haul off the trash that can make home life odious. And I open the windows to love.

Reflection

Think of a time when you have hauled off trash in your own life and opened the windows to love. How did it feel? What helped you get there? How can you get there again? How can you make that experience more common for you?

Applying this Strategy

☐ I don't think this will work for me.

☐ This is something I am already good at and use regularly to good effect.

☐ This is something I haven't tried but would like to try.

Next time [insert your parenting dilemma] happens, I'm going to try [insert your personal solution that applies this strategy].

Write a plan.

Visualize yourself doing it.

☐ This is something I have tried but need to practice.

Next time [insert your parenting dilemma] happens, I'm going to try [insert your personal solution that applies this strategy].

Write a plan.

Visualize yourself doing it.

Notes on progress: _____

_____

_____

_____

_____

33.

In Tough Times, Keep on Loving

Some time ago a mother asked my counsel about her 2nd grade daughter who was constantly in trouble at school for lying and for not cooperating well with classmates. In the oft-repeated scenario, the daughter would break a rule and, when confronted, would lie and get in trouble with her teacher. When she would not fess up, she was passed on to her counselor, her vice principal, and finally her principal. Then she came home to be in trouble with Mom.

After two years of this, Mom was fed up. She told me that she has met repeatedly with school professionals and they have not been able to find anything that works to curb the girl's lying.

The mother turned to me for guidance. I suggested to the mom that this little girl wanted more than anything else to be loved, to be safe, to be cherished. She isn't very skillful at winning good will. She gets crosswise of the system and, in a panic, she tells a story to try to avoid trouble. Then all the adults get indignant: "How could you lie? Do you think we're stupid enough to believe you?" And the little girl feels hopeless and desolate. She tells another tall tale in order to win the good will she desperately craves. All the adults get madder still.

What kind of person was the 2nd grader who was chronically in trouble for lying? When we visited her home, she excitedly showed us her brother's gerbils. She wanted to be helpful. She spoke excitedly of books she was reading. She wanted friendship and good will. The good news was that she was still trying very hard to win the good will of the people around her. That takes a lot of courage for a child who is in so much trouble so much of the time.

One of the great surprises in our experience as foster parents was that many of our foster children *defined* truth as that set of statements that was most likely to keep them out of trouble. At first we were indignant with their "lies." With time we learned to appreciate the life experiences that had led them to that point.

I suggested that, when the daughter tells a story, we don't need to get stuck in lectures on lying. Neither should the adults accept the story as truth; we can recognize it as a story. "Wow. That is a great story. I'm sure you wish it happened that way so that people would not be mad at you." "You and I both wish that were true. It would make life so much more pleasant." There must be no trace of irony or accusation, certainly no sarcasm. While there is no mistake in anyone's mind that the story is an invention, it is not necessarily a sign of a permanently sick and warped child. The first job is to do no harm.

Our second (and perhaps most challenging) job is to understand what the storytelling means to the child. We cannot help a child whom we have tidily categorized as bad. For the child, storytelling can actually be an attempt to create a harmony with fantasy that she does not know how to create with her behavior.

Storytelling can be a useful skill. She can be invited to tell the story that the principal experienced, the teacher experienced, that the wronged classmate experienced. Creativity should be cherished and nurtured—at the same time that truth-telling is cultivated.

I think that little girl was crying out in desperation, "Will someone please love me and understand me? I want to be a good kid but I keep doing dumb things and I keep getting in trouble. I am all mixed up. Can anyone see beyond my mistakes to a frightened child who wants to be loved and taught?"

I suggested to the mother that she could make sure that the problems at school did not cause a total eclipse of the child. Mom could fill her mind with the child's finest moments so that she is prepared to hug, cherish, and play with this struggling child. That little girl is begging for love but doing all the things that guarantee that she will get judgment, accusation, and punishment. As adults we need to break the cycle. We need to get out of our automatic reactions and answer that little girl's plea with healing balm. Along the way we teach her skills for dealing with situations that are currently overwhelming her.

Before we left the home, we witnessed that little girl reading a story to her mom that she had written and illustrated. It was amazing. This little girl wrote intelligently, read beautifully, and illustrated wonderfully. She was happy in this one little area where she is still able to succeed. That little island of competence should be cherished and enlarged through adult help.

Incidentally, there is more than lying that might help us "classify" that little girl. When she was two years old, she was at home with her mother who had come home from a dental appointment with a headache. While that little girl played, her mother, who had a chronic disease, died of an unusual reaction to the dental anesthetic. When Dad called home, it was that little girl who had to say, "Daddy, I can't wake Mommy up."

After her mother died, the little girl was raised primarily by her grandmother since her dad worked long hours and traveled. Then Grandma died. Then Dad remarried. In addition to an older sister, that girl now had two older stepsiblings who generally found her to be a nuisance. That is a lot of history for a six-year-old to sort out. That is a lot of life to shoulder with her small frame.

I don't know how her life history made her both desperate for love and willing to tell stories to keep from disappointing people, but we hardly need to be surprised. What that little girl needs is not careful analysis as much as patient compassion. There is no great lecture or any system of consequences that would help that little girl stop lying. But there is love.

Reflection

Think of a time when you have loved through the childrearing difficulties. How did it feel? What helped you get there? How can you get there again? How can you make that experience more common for you?

Applying this Strategy

☐ I don't think this will work for me.

☐ This is something I am already good at and use regularly to good effect.

☐ This is something I haven't tried but would like to try.

> Next time [insert your parenting dilemma] happens, I'm going to try [insert your personal solution that applies this strategy].
>
> > Write a plan.
> >
> > Visualize yourself doing it.

☐ This is something I have tried but need to practice.

> Next time [insert your parenting dilemma] happens, I'm going to try [insert your personal solution that applies this strategy].
>
> > Write a plan.
> >
> > Visualize yourself doing it.

Notes on progress: _____

_____

_____

_____

_____

34.

Teach Rather than Preach

Preaching has an impatient, condescending spirit to it. Teaching is different. It is about sharing and discovery. It honors the learner as an essential contributor.

Consider the importance of teaching social skills. Children who tend to get rejected at school are those who don't understand the rules of social interaction. A boy with that deficiency might try to enter a play group by grabbing a toy from one of his classmates. This does not endear him to the other children. He is further scorned and rejected.

In contrast, popular children who want to join a play group are likely to stand at the periphery of play. When they see a way to help—maybe one of the children drops a toy—the popular child jumps to help. That person is welcomed into the circle of friendship.

How did the popular child learn this skill? Did a parent sit down and provide instruction on methods for entering play groups? Maybe. It is also likely that the popular child saw those methods used at home. The child may also have been taught how to welcome friends into their home, how to share with siblings, and how to deal with differences.

What a tragedy that so many children do not have anyone to teach them! In our roles as parents, neighbors, and teachers, we have the opportunity to reach out to the untrained children and help them find ways to be a part of our little communities of love.

A good friend told me about a time when she taught her son. During their drive home from church, one son got mad at his brother. He got so mad that he called him foul names. Mom was mortified and angry. As they pulled up to the house she told the offending son that she was so angry that she didn't trust herself right then to respond to him appropriately. She asked him to go to his room to settle down while she went to hers. He was worried.

After giving herself a moment to soothe her anger, Mom went to her son's room. He was very humble. (He may also have been afraid for his life!) She explained to him why the language he had used was so troublesome to her. He apologized. She told him that he had also offended his brother. With her help, he went and apologized to his brother. When they returned to his room, he was right with his family and he was better prepared for future encounters. That mom wisely taught more than she preached.

Reflection

Think of a time when you have patiently and lovingly taught your child. How did it feel? What helped you get there? How can you get there again? How can you make that experience more common for you?

Applying this Strategy

☐ I don't think this will work for me.

☐ This is something I am already good at and use regularly to good effect.

☐ This is something I haven't tried but would like to try.

    Next time [insert your parenting dilemma] happens, I'm going to try [insert your personal solution that applies this strategy].

        Write a plan.

        Visualize yourself doing it.

☐ This is something I have tried but need to practice.

    Next time [insert your parenting dilemma] happens, I'm going to try [insert your personal solution that

applies this strategy].

    Write a plan.

    Visualize yourself doing it.

Notes on progress: _____

_____

_____

_____

_____

35.

Give Fair Warning

Haim Ginott made an astute observation about parental anger: "When we lose our temper, we act as though we have lost our sanity. We say and do things to our children that we would hesitate to inflict on an enemy. We yell, insult, and hit below the belt. When the fanfare is over, we feel guilty and we solemnly resolve never to render a repeat performance. But anger soon strikes again, undoing our good intentions. Once more we lash out at those to whose welfare we have dedicated our life and fortune."[39]

Ginott made recommendations for preventing the devastation of anger. He suggested that we express our irritation without attacking the child's personality or character. We can say things like:

> "I feel annoyed."
> "I feel irritated."
> "I am filled with indignation."
> "Right now I am very upset."

Sometimes just the statement of our feelings stops the bothersome behavior. Sometimes we may need to give more detail:

> "When I see shoes, socks, and shirts spread all over the floor, I get frustrated. I'm tempted to yell. I feel like opening the window and throwing the whole mess into the middle of the street."
> "It makes me upset to see you hit your brother. I can never allow you to hurt him."
> "When I see all of you rush away from dinner to watch TV, and leave me with the dirty dishes and greasy pans, I

feel upset! I fume inside! I need some help."

"When I call you for dinner and you don't come, I feel indignant. I say to myself, 'I cooked a good meal and I want some appreciation, not frustration.'"

Soft-spoken parents can be clear about their feelings without losing their tempers or attacking children. In fact, one of the best ways of preventing irrational anger is the expression of irritation long before it grows into anger.

Reflection

Think of a time when you have given fair warning, when you have expressed irritation before it became anger. How did it feel? What helped you get there? How can you get there again? How can you make that experience more common for you?

Applying this Strategy

☐ I don't think this will work for me.

☐ This is something I am already good at and use regularly to good effect.

☐ This is something I haven't tried but would like to try.

> Next time [insert your parenting dilemma] happens, I'm going to try [insert your personal solution that applies this strategy].
>
> Write a plan.
>
> Visualize yourself doing it.

☐ This is something I have tried but need to practice.

> Next time [insert your parenting dilemma] happens, I'm going to try [insert your personal solution that applies this strategy].
>
> Write a plan.
>
> Visualize yourself doing it.

Notes on progress: _____

_____

_____

_____

_____

36.

Keep the Ratio Right

John Gottman[40] may be the world's leading marriage researcher. In his extensive studies of couples, he has found a magic ratio. In couple relationships that are strong, there are five positives for each negative. If you want a strong relationship, it is not enough to deliver one positive for each negative. It takes five positives for each negative. That is one of the best ways to assure a strong and enduring relationship.

Virginia Williams has applied this same idea to raising children. She suggests that many children hear a steady stream of complaints, accusations, and acrimony. The children who become healthy adults are more likely to grow in a lake of support, encouragement, and appreciation.

If we monitored our messages to our children, I'm afraid that most of us would fall short of the magic ratio. Many of us deliver far too many corrections, irritations, and reprimands. Children's energetic spirits may be crushed under the weight of our negativity.

But we can change. We can be more mindful of the climate of our relationship with each child. We can offer more sunshine than storm. We can take our frustrations out on exercise rather than on our children. We can look for the good and talk about it.

Our goal is to have five positives for each negative.

Reflection: Think of a time when you have given far more positives than negatives to each of your children. How did it feel? What helped you get there? How can you get there again? How can you make that experience more common for you?

Applying this Strategy

☐ I don't think this will work for me.

☐ This is something I am already good at and use regularly to good effect.

☐ This is something I haven't tried but would like to try.

> Next time [insert your parenting dilemma] happens, I'm going to try [insert your personal solution that applies this strategy].
>
> > Write a plan.
> >
> > Visualize yourself doing it.

☐ This is something I have tried but need to practice.

> Next time [insert your parenting dilemma] happens, I'm going to try [insert your personal solution that applies this strategy].
>
> > Write a plan.
> >
> > Visualize yourself doing it.

Notes on progress: _____

_____

_____

_____

_____

37.

Learn Your Children's Languages of Love

There is a trick to loving children effectively. Effective loving requires us to deliver what is important to the specific child we are loving. It is not enough to say, "I love you!"—even with gusto. We can tell a daughter that she is loved, but she may prefer that you play with her. We can tell our son he is loved, but he may prefer that you throw the ball with him. One child might want snuggling while another loves story time. Each child is different.

This complex challenge could almost seem discouraging—except there are such wonderful and natural ways to discover each child's native love language. Very often children tell us exactly what they want:

> "Please listen to me!"
> "Hurry! Come see the bug outside!"
> "Will you read me a story?"
> "Are you mad at me?"

In every request is a hint about that child's needs and interests. In every question is also a cry for reassurance.

Haim Ginott tells a great story about six-year-old Flora who complained that she had not been receiving as many presents as her brother. Mother did not argue with Flora's perception. She did not pull out her check register to prove otherwise. She did not justify any differences saying that her brother was older and so needed more presents. A wise mother knew that children are more concerned about the relationship than about the size and number of gifts. Mother simply said, "You wonder if I love you as much as him?" Without adding another word, mother hugged little Flora, who responded with a smile of surprise and pleasure. This was the right answer to a question that could have become an endless argument.

Flora wanted to be reassured that she was loved. Her mother was astute enough to recognize the real question behind the complaint. Mom answered the real question.

We can deliver the message in the way that works for each child. How can we know what each child wants? I suggest three ways:

1. We can notice what each child asks for.

2. We can notice how each child tends to show love.

3. We can notice what we have done in the past that seemed to be an effective message of love for that child.

I like to say that there are three particular languages of love and two universal ones.[41] The universal languages are taking time and being understanding. When someone spends time with us doing something we love to do, that sends a clear message of love. As to being understanding, when someone takes the time to really understand my feelings, I am warmed and comforted by that person's love and goodness.

The three particular languages of love are (1) show me, (2) tell me, and (3) touch me. Some children are only convinced that we love them when they see our actions (the *show me*'s). Some are dying to hear (or read) words of love (the *tell me*'s). Others want to snuggle (the *touch me*'s).

Of course every person has some unique combination of love languages. And they change from time to time. A child who is lonely and tired may want to snuggle even though that is not usually her language of love.

It is not enough to work hard at parenting. We must work smart. Learning to express love in the customized ways our children prefer is one of the smartest things a parent can do.

Reflection

Think of a time when you have shown love to each of your children in a way that really communicated to that child. How did it feel? What helped you get there? How can you get there again? How can you make that experience more common for you?

Applying this Strategy

☐ I don't think this will work for me.

☐ This is something I am already good at and use regularly to good effect.

☐ This is something I haven't tried but would like to try.

    Next time [insert your parenting dilemma] happens, I'm going to try [insert your personal solution that applies this strategy].

        Write a plan.

        Visualize yourself doing it.

☐ This is something I have tried but need to practice.

    Next time [insert your parenting dilemma] happens, I'm going to try [insert your personal solution that applies this strategy].

        Write a plan.

        Visualize yourself doing it.

Notes on progress: _____

_____

_____

_____

_____

38.

Enrich Your Parenting

We seem to assume that parenting should just come naturally. We surely don't want to admit to friends or neighbors that we are bewildered or vexed by the challenges of raising children.

What a crazy assumption! Nothing is more challenging than parenting. It is one of the most challenging courses that life offers. It is extraordinarily rare for anyone to make an A in this course!

Yet we do not attend lectures, hold study groups, or read books to help us pass the tests of parenting. No wonder that we fail so many parenting tests!

I recommend that *every* parent do several things:

1. Read the best books on parenting.[42] Following are some suggestions:

> *Between Parent and Child* by Haim Ginott
> *Raising an Emotionally Intelligent Child* by John Gottman
> *How to Talk So Kids will Listen and Listen So Kids Will Talk* by Adele Faber and Elaine Mazlish

For parents of newborns:

> *What to Expect the First Year* by Arlene Eisenberg & Assoc.
> *Dr. Spock's Baby and Child Care* by Benjamin Spock and Michael Rothenberg

2. Take good classes when they are offered.

Unfortunately, there are far more poor books and classes than good ones. How can you tell the difference? Generally, the best ones are sponsored by universities or other groups that are less commercial and more research-based. Also, the best ones encourage you to show love to your children while helping them cultivate their agency. Any program that encourages harsh or manipulative parenting should be avoided. Be cautious about any programs that offer sure cures. Life doesn't offer simple, guaranteed formulas. We always must use wisdom and good sense. Any parenting guru who offers sure cures is unwise and probably hawking a poor program.

3. Interview parents you respect.

You probably know some parents who seem to have a knack for raising children. Watch them for ideas. Interview them. Ask them what they have learned. Ask them how they deal with challenging situations. You might even set up a discussion group in which they share ideas with conscientious parents.

4. Draw on wisdom literature.

Every year there is a new crop of wonder-books. While our understanding of parenting continues to evolve, there are timeless truths that can help us. You may find your inspiration in the Bible, the Torah, the Upanishads, the Koran, or Greek philosophy.

I personally find the teachings of Jesus to be some of the most humanizing and wise counsel I have found anywhere. Wherever you find timeless truth, cherish it.

5. Get help from others.

We cannot raise children effectively without help. You may have a parenting partner who is your perfect balance. You may be a single parent with capable and compassionate extended family. Or you may be a person who carefully draws capable and caring adults into your children's lives. No parent can do the job alone. We should all draw into our children's lives those good people who will provide them experiences that we are not able to.

6. Share your successes and struggles with other parents.

As you share your experiences in parenting with other parents you will cultivate a support group that can help you and other members of the group.

Reflection

Think of a time when you have gained from sharing with other parents. What helped you get there? How can you get there again? Is there anything you can do to make that experience more common for you?

Applying this Strategy

☐ I don't think this will work for me.
☐ This is something I am already good at and use regularly to good effect.
☐ This is something I haven't tried but would like to try.
> Next time [insert your parenting dilemma] happens, I'm going to try [insert your personal solution that applies this strategy].
>> Write a plan.
>> Visualize yourself doing it.

☐ This is something I have tried but need to practice.
> Next time [insert your parenting dilemma] happens, I'm going to try [insert your personal solution that applies this strategy].
>> Write a plan.
>> Visualize yourself doing it.

Notes on progress: _____

_____

_____

_____

_____

39.

Set Yourself up for Success

We often set ourselves and our children up for failure. We expect perfect performance. We don't allow time for unexpected challenges. We drag around with us loads of irritation from all areas of life. It's no wonder that we blow up when our children do something "annoying."

We can choose a different course. We can set ourselves up for success. John Covey, a friend and colleague, told me about coming home from work feeling tired. Before he entered the house to greet Jane and their children, he paused in the car and refocused. He asked Heaven for the energy and goodness to enter family life as a source of light. He planned ahead and chose a different course.

If we leave delicate or dangerous things where children can reach them, we are courting disaster. Child-proofing our homes is one way of setting ourselves up for success. We put some things out of reach of children. But we can go a step farther. We can do child-fitting in our homes. We can be sure there are toys and activities available that *are* appropriate for children. We can have puzzles, blocks, and balls available that will keep children busy and happy.

There are more ways to set ourselves up for success. When we make trips in the car, we make sure children have toys to play with. When we take children to the store, we provide them things to do or ways to help. When it is almost time for bed, we give children warning—maybe we set a timer—so they don't have a meltdown when the time comes.

James D. Stice, a management professor, tells of setting up his daughter for success.[43]

I have a six-year-old daughter named Cierra. Her favorite thing to do is play dress-up with her friends. When I walk into the house, I never know what my role is to be. She, with her friends Madison and Bethany, may be Snow White or Ariel or Jasmine or Sleeping Beauty—otherwise known as Princess Aurora—and I may instantly be called on to be Prince Eric or King Triton or Gaston or the wicked Jafar. I must always be on my toes because these girls take their game seriously. They don't like it when an amateur messes up his lines.

I went into Cierra's room at the end of a recent hard day of playing dress-up. It looked like a Disney Store had exploded. There were outfits everywhere, with props all over the place. I went in search of the princess because someone was going to clean up this mess, and that someone was not going to be me. I found Cierra and calmly explained to her the situation and my concern. She immediately understood and headed to her room to take care of the problem. After five minutes I went to her room—her still messy room—to find her playing with her Barbies. I asked what she was doing, and she said, as though I was a bit slow, "I'm playing Barbies."

"But, Cierra," I said, "I thought you were going to clean up this room."

She said to me, "But, Daddy, there is too much stuff out. Besides, I didn't make this whole mess by myself."

I then explained to her that she should have thought of that when she and her friends were making the mess. "Now clean up this mess," I sternly declared.

I went back every five minutes or so to make sure she was staying on task, and, bless her heart, she kept trying. But the mess was too big for her. After all, three little girls together make a much bigger mess than three little girls individually. There is some synergy there.

After a half-hour of periodically checking on her and verbally poking her to keep her working, I again went into her room only to find her lying on her bed with her back to the door. I marched over to the bed thinking she had gone to sleep. How dare she do that! Just as I reached down to turn her over, she rolled back and, with big, tear-filled brown eyes, said, "Daddy, it's too hard."

The weight of a six-year-old's world can get very heavy— to a six-year-old. She did not want to hear me say, "I could clean this room up in five minutes" or "When I was your age . . ." At that moment the weight was too much, and she needed relief. So Prince Eric picked her up, and he, together with Princess Ariel, cleaned up the castle. It didn't take much effort on my part to lighten a load that to her had become too heavy.

So we can become soft-spoken and effective parents when we make allowances for unexpected challenges and childish balkiness.

Reflection

Think of a time when you have set yourself and your children up for success. How did it feel? What helped you get there? How can you get there again? How can you make that experience more common for you?

Applying this Strategy

☐ I don't think this will work for me.

☐ This is something I am already good at and use regularly to good effect.

☐ This is something I haven't tried but would like to try.

> Next time [insert your parenting dilemma] happens, I'm going to try [insert your personal solution that applies this strategy].
>
> > Write a plan.
> >
> > Visualize yourself doing it.

☐ This is something I have tried but need to practice.

> Next time [insert your parenting dilemma] happens, I'm going to try [insert your personal solution that applies this strategy].
>
> > Write a plan.
> >
> > Visualize yourself doing it.

Notes on progress: _____

_____

_____

_____

_____

40.

Change Your View of Children and Human Nature

We all make certain assumptions about people and the reasons they do the things they do. We call this an implicit personality theory. Tucked away in our personal theories are ideas about the basic goodness and badness of people. Here are voices of three different views of human nature:

1. Children are basically bad.

John Calvin (16th Century): Children's whole nature is a certain seed of Sin, therefore it cannot but be hateful and abominable to God.[44]

Sigmund Freud (19th and 20th Centuries): I have found little that is good about human beings. In my experience most of them are trash. . . . In the depths of my heart, I can't help being convinced that my dear fellowmen, with few exceptions, are worthless.[45]

Anna Freud (20th Century): From birth onwards, children feel the pressure of urgent body needs and powerful instinctive urges (such as hunger, sex, aggression) which clamor for satisfaction.[46]

John Rosemond (20th and 21st Centuries): Give your children regular and realistic doses of Vitamin N ("no"). When you do, and they fall to the floor screaming, pat yourself on the back for a job well done. Remember that sufficient exposure to frustration not only prepares a child for the reality of adulthood, but gradually helps the child develop a tolerance for frustration.[47]

This is a gloomy view of human nature. It can lead to negative parenting. Of course there is some truth to it. Children—and all humans—

sometimes act in selfish ways. But it probably isn't the most important part of human nature.

2. Children are clay.

Aristotle (300 BC): The soul of a child is like a clean slate on which nothing is written, on it you may write what you will.[48]

John B. Watson (20th Century): Give me a dozen healthy infants, well-formed, and my own specified world to bring them up in and I'll guarantee to take any one at random and train him to become any type of specialist I might select—into a doctor, lawyer, artist, merchant-chief, and yes, even into beggar-man and thief, regardless of his talents, penchants, tendencies, abilities, vocations and race of ancestors.[49]

This view assumes that children are merely mercenaries. You can get them to do anything with the right reward. It has an element of truth. We can get children to become little terrorists when that is the only way they can get our attention. But this view certainly does not explain all of human nature. Could we have turned Mother Teresa into a mugger by regularly rewarding bad behavior? I don't think so.

3. Children are good, innocent, angelic.

Rousseau (18th Century): All things are good as they come out of the hands of the Creator, but everything degenerates in the hands of man.[50]

Harry Emerson Fosdick (20th Century): Every exaltation, every pure sentiment, all urgency of true affection, and all yearning after things higher and nobler, are testimonies of the divinity that is in us.[51]

Abraham Maslow (20th Century): If one looks at a healthy and well-loved and cared-for infant . . . then it is quite impossible to see anything that could be called evil. . . . On the contrary, careful and long-continued observation demonstrates the opposite. Practically every personality characteristic found in [the most exemplary] people, everything lovable, admirable, and enviable is found in babies.[52]

Our view of children and their nature affects the way we treat them. While they may act basically bad when they are tired and frustrated and may act like clay when they want something from us, the most interesting and powerful part of human nature is the noble within them. Each human being is a miracle of creation.

So, when children are cranky, we soothe them. When they act like little mercenaries, we make sure we are not rewarding bad behavior. But the heart of effective parenting is encouraging the nobility in each child. By noticing, encouraging and celebrating the good in children's natures, we make it the central theme of their characters.

Reflection

Think of a time when you have taken a positive view of your children. How did it feel? What helped you get there? How can you get there again? How can you make that experience more common for you?

Applying this Strategy

☐ I don't think this will work for me.

☐ This is something I am already good at and use regularly to good effect.

☐ This is something I haven't tried but would like to try.

> Next time [insert your parenting dilemma] happens, I'm going to try [insert your personal solution that applies this strategy].
>> Write a plan.
>> Visualize yourself doing it.

☐ This is something I have tried but need to practice.

Next time [insert your parenting dilemma] happens,
I'm going to try [insert your personal solution that
applies this strategy].

    Write a plan.

    Visualize yourself doing it.

Notes on progress: _____

_____

_____

_____

_____

41.

Use Persuasion

Certain words and phrases come quite naturally to most parents, ie., "You'll do it because I say so!" While these words may cop reluctant compliance, they do not educate either the child's mind or heart.

Persuasion is better. One evening years ago Nancy was away at a meeting and I was watching the children. While I was washing the dishes I did not notice the great danger sign familiar to all mothers: the kids were quiet. When I finished the dishes, I entered the family room to find that Andy had discovered the finger paints on the bottom shelf of the bookcase. The bold swatches of brilliant red, yellow, green, and blue were breathtaking on our new carpet.

On that occasion I was calm enough to consider: "What does this mean to Andy? Is he trying to torment me? No. Is he merely exploring and enjoying his childish world? I think so." So I explained to him the disadvantage of painting on carpet: "People will spoil your art by walking on it." I explained the advantage of finger-painting on slick paper that can be hung on the fridge. "Grandma will keep it forever!"

"Ohhhhh!" said Andy in a delighted way. He understood. And we cleaned up the carpet together.

Persuasion is the gentle art of helping children to learn and behave without being humiliated. This approach is endorsed by decades of parenting. The best way to influence children is with a method we call induction,[53] which is when we reason with children and help them understand how their behavior affects others. This kind of parenting helps children become strong and caring adults.

There is a way in which this point is commonly misunderstood. Some parents feel that they must continue to cajole and beg their children until their children agree with them. They seem very intimidated about the prospect of having their children unhappy with them. This is not persuasion. This is intimidation by children.

The wise parent works to educate a child without giving in to a child's browbeating. Obviously this is a fine art which, when mastered, pays off with both more family peace and children who enjoy both confidence and sensitivity.

Reflection

Think of a time when you have used persuasion with one of your children. How did it feel? What helped you get there? How can you get there again? How can you make that experience more common for you?

Applying this Strategy

- [ ] I don't think this will work for me.
- [ ] This is something I am already good at and use regularly to good effect.
- [ ] This is something I haven't tried but would like to try.
    Next time [insert your parenting dilemma] happens, I'm going to try [insert your personal solution that applies this strategy].
        Write a plan.
        Visualize yourself doing it.
- [ ] This is something I have tried but need to practice.
    Next time [insert your parenting dilemma] happens, I'm going to try [insert your personal solution that applies this strategy].
        Write a plan.
        Visualize yourself doing it.

Notes on progress: _____

_____

_____

_____

_____

42.

Invest 5 Minutes to Save an Hour

My esteemed colleague, Karen DeBord, suggests that parents can often invest five minutes to save an hour. This is especially true when we have been away from our children for some time. They miss us. If we invest a few minutes reading, cuddling, listening, talking, walking, or rocking, we may save an evening of nagging and battles—and a lifetime of distance.

Nancy knew how to use this principle with our dear daughter, Sara, when she was a teen. When Nancy wanted to connect with Sara, she knew that she could not just offer a quick hello or a few words of affection. It takes a few minutes to reconnect.

So Nancy would take Sara with her to run errands. As they rode along in the car, Sara moved from superficial talk to cautious probing to soul sharing. It was simply the best way to reconnect with Sara.

A good mom in Montgomery, Alabama once asked me how to deal with her sullen teen. The girl was often disagreeable, but when she first came home from school each day she wanted to spend some time hugging her mama. The mom was okay with a quick hug. But the daughter wanted to hang on. It drove the mother crazy. She had much to do. She figured a quick hug should do the job.

I encouraged the mother to mentally plan to take a few minutes to hug her daughter any time the daughter wanted a hug. Just be there. Take as many minutes as the daughter wanted.

The mother tried it. She discovered two surprises. First, contrary to expectation, the daughter did not lean on her for hours. After only a minute or two, the daughter was happy and went about her business. The second surprise was that those few minutes made a real difference in the quality of the remaining hours of the day.

As the Spanish proverb observes, "An ounce of mother is worth a ton of priest."

Reflection

Think of a time when you have invested a few minutes to reconnect with one of your children. How did it feel? What helped you make the investment? How can you do it again? How can you make that experience more common for you?

Applying this Strategy

☐ I don't think this will work for me.

☐ This is something I am already good at and use regularly to good effect.

☐ This is something I haven't tried but would like to try.

    Next time [insert your parenting dilemma] happens, I'm going to try [insert your personal solution that applies this strategy].

        Write a plan.

        Visualize yourself doing it.

☐ This is something I have tried but need to practice.

    Next time [insert your parenting dilemma] happens, I'm going to try [insert your personal solution that applies this strategy].

        Write a plan.

        Visualize yourself doing it.

Notes on progress: _____

_____

_____

_____

_____

_____

43.

Make Repairs

We all get mad. We all hurt each other. We all have regular need of repentance.

One evening my daughter Sara and I were competing at some game. Sara is very good at games. But I was quite determined to do my best in this competition. I wanted to win.

In the process I was not very kind. When Sara's feeling were hurt, I blamed her for starting a game she wasn't willing to lose. Each of us felt offended by the other.

I did not sleep well that night. In the middle of the night I wandered to the livings room and sat in the hint of moonlight rocking in a chair. When sleep would not come, I chose to use the time to ponder. I asked myself, "What do I need to do to be a better family member?"

Immediately the experience with Sara earlier that evening came to mind. I realized that I needed to set things right with Sara. Since she was long-since asleep, I put a chair in the hall outside her room, placed a teddy bear on the chair, and left a note in the hands of the bear telling her how sorry I was that I had been unkind. I love Sara more than life itself and know I am foolish when I let anything blind me to that love. I told her just that.

All of us have occasion to make repairs in our relationships with our children. They will respect and love us more as they witness us apologize for our follies. In addition, they will become better at making repairs themselves.

Reflection

Think of a time when you have made repairs in a relationship with one of your children. How did it feel? What helped you get there? How can you get there again? How can you make that experience more common for you?

Applying this Strategy

☐ I don't think this will work for me.

☐ This is something I am already good at and use regularly to good effect.

☐ This is something I haven't tried but would like to try.

> Next time [insert your parenting dilemma] happens, I'm going to try [insert your personal solution that applies this strategy].
>
>> Write a plan.
>>
>> Visualize yourself doing it.

☐ This is something I have tried but need to practice.

> Next time [insert your parenting dilemma] happens, I'm going to try [insert your personal solution that applies this strategy].
>
>> Write a plan.
>>
>> Visualize yourself doing it.

Notes on progress: _____

_____

_____

_____

_____

44.

Give Choices

One of the primary objectives of good parenting is teaching children how to use their agency (or decision-making power) wisely. We don't accomplish that purpose when we make all their decisions for them. We also don't help them when we leave them to make decisions for which they are not prepared. For that reason, one of our family mottoes is:

> It is our job to help our children get what they want in a
> way we feel good about.

Notice the two parts of this formula:

1. We want to help them get what they want. We want them to have experience, growth, and lots of freedom.

2. We should set bounds on their decisions so they are not required to make decisions for which they are not prepared.

Just as we must learn to act within reasonable bounds, so we should teach our children to act within the reasonable bounds we set.

Tommy was sitting on my lap as I read a book to him. After we had read for a while he seemed to become bored. He got a pencil and looked like he was going to write in the book. His dad jumped at him, grabbed the pencil, and shouted, "You do not write in books!" Both Tommy and I were shocked.

I think it would have been more helpful to give Tommy a choice. The father could ask him, "Would you like to draw? We don't draw in books but I can get you some paper to draw on. Or would you like to finish the book?" Either choice would have been fine.[54]

Sometimes children resist us because we try to force them to do things. When we do not give them choices, they are more likely to rebel. A young child may resist going to bed. We may try to force the child. But they can resist us with calls for water, and a light, and a story. We can hurl angry lectures and threats at them.

It may be better to give choices. We might ask, "Would you like daddy or mommy to tuck you in?" or "Would you like to pick a storybook for me to read to you or would you like me to pick one?" If the child says that she does not want to go to bed, we can ask the same question. She has a choice within boundaries set by her parents. We can be perfectly pleasant while being totally firm.

Of course we should only give children choices when we feel that either choice is acceptable. We do not let a small child decide to play with knives or run into traffic. Adult wisdom should frame choices for children. But we should allow children to pick the shirt they will wear even if it has a bit of mustard on it.

As children become teens, many conflicts arise out of differences in taste. We interpret their style in clothes or music to suggest disrespect or rebellion. Sometimes it does. Often it does not.

In matters of style, it is better not to start a battle. We may think our child's hair is too long or too short or that baggy pants look ridiculous. (Probably our parents had some of the same concerns about our style.) We allow our children freedom to express themselves in ways that are not unsafe or immoral. We try not to panic when some of those choices are different from ones we would make.

It is not helpful to pester children, but we can help them learn sensible ways of making choices. If we want our children to be good decision-makers when they become adults, we should give them many appropriate opportunities to make decisions along their journey to adulthood.

When Andy seemed to play music from the band U2 endlessly, I was tempted to tell him to shut off his stinking music. Instead, I gave him a choice. I asked if he would rather play the music quietly or use headsets. (The irony is that I now own and enjoy several U2 albums.)

If we want our children to become good decision-makers, we should give them lots of chances to make choices—within reasonable bounds.

Reflection

Think of a time when you have appropriately allowed your children to make choices. How did it feel? What helped you get there? How can you get there again? How can you make that experience more common for you?

Applying this Strategy

☐ I don't think this will work for me.

☐ This is something I am already good at and use regularly to good effect.

☐ This is something I haven't tried but would like to try.

    Next time [insert your parenting dilemma] happens, I'm going to try [insert your personal solution that applies this strategy].

        Write a plan.

        Visualize yourself doing it.

☐ This is something I have tried but need to practice.

    Next time [insert your parenting dilemma] happens, I'm going to try [insert your personal solution that applies this strategy].

        Write a plan.

        Visualize yourself doing it.

Notes on progress: _____

_____

_____

_____

_____

45.

Turn It Over to a Rule

It is quite possible to have endless battles over trivial matters. For example, how many arguments have there been over coats since Mother Eve told Seth to bundle up and button up when he went out to play? We describe the catastrophes that await children who do not dress warmly. Yet children insist that they are not cold.

It does not make sense to argue with someone else's perception. How can we settle this timeless battle?

One method is to let a rule speak for us. Maybe we make the rule that a jacket or coat must be worn if the temperature is below 50 degrees. As a child is dashing out the door to school, we can remind the child to grab a coat. If they resist, we point them to the rule: "Check the thermometer. Over 50, you decide. Below 50, wrap up tight."

In many cases we can let consequences teach children. Mother nature is one of the best teachers in the universe. A child who doesn't wear a coat may get chilly. A child who refuses sunscreen may get sunburned. We can let her do a lot of the teaching. A healthy child is likely to survive outdoor play in temperatures that might bother us.

In situations where there are genuine safety concerns, we can point children to simple rules. In other situations, the children may decide.

Reflection

Think of a time when you have pointed your children to a simple rule. How did it work? What helped you form and use the rule? How can you minimize conflict by appropriate use of rules?

Applying this Strategy

☐ I don't think this will work for me.

☐ This is something I am already good at and use regularly to good effect.

☐ This is something I haven't tried but would like to try.

> Next time [insert your parenting dilemma] happens, I'm going to try [insert your personal solution that applies this strategy].
>
> > Write a plan.
> >
> > Visualize yourself doing it.

☐ This is something I have tried but need to practice.

> Next time [insert your parenting dilemma] happens, I'm going to try [insert your personal solution that applies this strategy].
>
> > Write a plan.
> >
> > Visualize yourself doing it.

Notes on progress: _____

_____

_____

_____

_____

46.

Respond to Anger with Compassion

"If we practice an eye for an eye and a tooth for a tooth, soon we will all be blind and toothless," Mahatma Gandhi observed. Jesus asked us to live by a higher standard than the Law of Moses: "But I say unto you, Love your enemies, bless them that curse you, do good to them that hate you, and pray for them which despitefully use you, and persecute you."[55]

When our children are upset with us, we don't have to become defensive. We can show compassion for their pain—even when we cannot agree to their wishes.

John Gottman tells the story of flying home from a visit with relatives with his daughter, two-year-old Moriah who was bored, tired, and cranky.[56] Moriah asked for Zebra, her favorite stuffed animal. Unfortunately Zebra was packed in the suitcase in the hold of the plane.

John explained to his tired girl that he could not get Zebra—that he was in a suitcase under the plane.

Did Moriah say to herself, "Too bad. I'm disappointed, but I might as well relax"? No. She whined pitifully for her stuffed animal.

Once again Dad explained the situation and apologized. Moriah's moans turned to screams. "I want Zebra! I want Zebra!"

At this point many of us are tempted to lose our cool. We have been civil, why can't the child be civil? In fact, her dad's blood pressure was rising. He explained again and offered another toy. Moriah got more upset, "*I want Zebra!*"

Out of desperation, Gottman turned to the very thing he recommends to parents. He offered her compassion. He moved out of his defenses into her yearning. "You wish you had Zebra right now."

"Yeah," replied Moriah.

"You're tired and you would like to snuggle with Zebra and feel him against your face. You'd like to get out of these seats and climb into your big, soft bed full of all your stuffed animals."

"Yeah."

"I wish we could, too. I would love to snuggle with you and read you a story like we often do." Moriah began to relax. Soon she was asleep.

Gottman followed Ginott's wise prescription: Grant in fantasy what you cannot grant in reality. Gottman could not get Zebra for Moriah. And Moriah did not want explanations. She wanted compassion. When Dad stopped pushing back on her request and stood with her (emotionally) to understand her request, she became more peaceful.

Compassion is a timeless gift. It is even more precious when children are upset.

Reflection

Think of a time when you have responded to a child's anger with compassion. How did it feel? What helped you get there? How can you get there again? How can you make that experience more common for you?

Applying this Strategy

- [ ] I don't think this will work for me.
- [ ] This is something I am already good at and use regularly to good effect.

☐ This is something I haven't tried but would like to try.

    Next time [insert your parenting dilemma] happens, I'm going to try [insert your personal solution that applies this strategy].

        Write a plan.

        Visualize yourself doing it.

☐ This is something I have tried but need to practice.

    Next time [insert your parenting dilemma] happens, I'm going to try [insert your personal solution that applies this strategy].

        Write a plan.

        Visualize yourself doing it.

Notes on progress: _____

_____

_____

_____

_____

47.

Make Allowances for a Child's Childishness

It is natural—but not helpful—for us to impose grown-up expectations on little people. Haim Ginott recommends that we accept the childishness of children.[57] This means accepting that "a clean shirt on a normal child will not stay clean for long, that running rather than walking is the child's normal means of locomotion, that a tree is for climbing and a mirror is for making faces."

A mother called Nancy and me one day because her four-year-old girl was making her crazy. We asked for examples of the misbehavior that were upsetting Mama. Mom fumed, "Sometimes Julie leaves the hall light on in the day. Sometimes she even brings cookies into the living room."

Most of the "unpardonable sins" of childhood are merely a part of being a human—especially a human without a lot of experience. At what point in life should we expect people to reliably turn off the hall lights and leave cookies in the kitchen? I'm not sure. But it is a lot to ask of a four-year-old.

Rather than get mad when Julie forgets to turn off the light, a parent might say, "Julie, it looks like you forgot the light. Do you mind turning it off?" A parent can expect to do this about 1,700 times before the child does it without prompting.

Rather than become indignant when Julie brings a cookie into the living room, we might invite: "Do you want me to join you in the kitchen while you eat your cookie? I'd love to be with you. Or you can leave it in the kitchen to eat later."

I remember when our Emily was a little girl. She asked me to draw a circle for her. I thought that was goofy. "You're a smart girl! You can draw a circle. Just think of a cookie and draw it." A few days later I read that drawing circles is something that some children can't do until they are much older than Emily was. I was not making allowances for childishness.

Childishness is not a bad thing—in children. When we sign up for parenting, we should expect that we will be doing a lot of teaching, reminding—and forgiving.

Reflection

Think of a time when you have made allowances for childishness. How did it feel? What helped you get there? How can you get there again? How can you make that experience more common for you?

Applying this Strategy

☐ I don't think this will work for me.

☐ This is something I am already good at and use regularly to good effect.

☐ This is something I haven't tried but would like to try.

Next time [insert your parenting dilemma] happens, I'm going to try [insert your personal solution that applies this strategy].

Write a plan.

Visualize yourself doing it.

☐ This is something I have tried but need to practice.

Next time [insert your parenting dilemma] happens, I'm going to try [insert your personal solution that applies this strategy].

Write a plan.

Visualize yourself doing it.

Notes on progress: _____

_____

_____

_____

_____

48.

Be Strategic

Sometimes we become anything but soft-spoken when children do not respond to our requests. And we may have acted without considering what would help the child move in the desired direction. Sometimes we get just what we should have expected.

I like the story about a woman who stepped out of the house to throw something in the trash. When she returned to the house, she found that she was locked out. Inside was her four-year-old son. She could demand that her son open the door immediately. We all know what would happen. There would be a battle of wills with Mom increasing threats and son resisting demands. The mother chose to be strategic. In a sad voice she said, "Oh, too bad. You just locked yourself in the house." The boy opened the door at once.

That is being strategic! Rather than doing things that we know won't work, we can do the things that will work. For example, rushing and nagging children does not help them get ready for school on time. What is a more strategic approach? One mother told her sons that as soon as they were fully ready for school, they could watch cartoons until time to leave for school. A Dad motivated his children by having a hot breakfast for those who were ready on time. Those who were not got a granola bar.

A parent who had a hard time getting children dressed could play the role of a salesperson. "Sir, are you looking for something to wear today? We have two lovely shirts to choose from. Does one appeal to you? Would you also like a handsome pair of pants? We have this snappy blue pair and a casual brown pair. Which of these appeals to you?" The parent continues until the child is dressed, and then can conclude: "Thank you for shopping with us today." A hug and laugh would be a fitting conclusion. In those situations where this approach will work, it is certainly better than demanding and threatening.

A child who has a hard time sitting still at a school program, at church or in the doctor's office might benefit from some strategic parenting. A parent might draw pictures of activities that the child could do and invite the child to plan the time.

The child could help the parent pack the bag with supplies. Children are more likely to have a good experience if they help plan their experience.

There is even a strategic way of dealing with tantrums. When a child has a meltdown, the parent can sit nearby and wait with perfect tranquility. The parent can even say, "I sure want to hear your feelings. I can't understand what you're saying right now. When you're ready, please tell me what you're feeling." Then the parent waits for the child to calm down.

A parent can get children to eat better by making an adventure of it. "That broccoli looks like a tree. What does it taste like?" Parents can also use or provide a cookie cutter to form interesting shapes. And many of us have made ants on a log (peanut butter and raisins on celery). A child might also bring a stuffed animal to the table to "share" the meal with.

Any one of these ideas—or all of them—might not work for a given child. Fortunately, you are an expert on your children. You can design the strategic approaches that will work with each of your children. Whether it is happy ways to get hair washed or methods to help them fall asleep, being strategic can often help us keep our temper.[58]

Reflection

Think of a time when you have been strategic in dealing with your children. How did it feel? What helped you get there? How can you get there again?

How can you remember to use strategy rather than threats in the future?

Applying this Strategy

☐ I don't think this will work for me.

☐ This is something I am already good at and use regularly to good effect.

☐ This is something I haven't tried but would like to try.

> Next time [insert your parenting dilemma] happens, I'm going to try [insert your personal solution that applies this strategy].
>
>> Write a plan.
>>
>> Visualize yourself doing it.

☐ This is something I have tried but need to practice.

> Next time [insert your parenting dilemma] happens, I'm going to try [insert your personal solution that applies this strategy].
>
>> Write a plan.
>>
>> Visualize yourself doing it.

Notes on progress: _____

_____

_____

_____

_____

49.

Send a Clear Message

Often we send mixed messages to our children. We say things like "You're a nice kid *but* why don't you clean up your room, do your chores, help your brother, etc.?" That is one big "but."

One Saturday morning I was standing with a friend in the entrance to his garage.[59] As we spoke, his young son rode into the garage on his bike and parked it in front of their old station wagon. Something about parking the bike there violated a family rule because the father interrupted our conversation to launch over to his son, grab him, hold him up in the air, and start to yell the Standard Parental Lecture. "Why do you always. . . . Why can't you ever. . . . Won't you ever learn. . . . What is it going to take. . . . "

Let's leave our adult perspective and see the situation from the child's point of view. What do you think the son was thinking as he was suspended in mid-air with an angry face belching his mistakes? Do you think he was saying, "I am so glad that dad is bringing these things to my attention. This will really help me to be more responsible."

I don't think so. I don't think the boy was doing any quiet reflecting. I suspect that he was mostly feeling. Fear. Anger. Humiliation. Hurt. If my discernment is correct, the boy was submissive on the outside but hurt and angry on the inside.

When the father had finished his harangue, he paused, still panting from the angry lecture. Then he bellowed, "I love you." He set his son down and returned to pick up the conversation with me.

Again, let's take the child's perspective. Do you think the boy felt loved?

Do you think he felt safe and cherished? I don't think so. I think he was hurt. The person who should be his friend, protector, teacher, and advocate had acted with disregard for him and his feelings. The father had expressed his own anger. Even though he loved his son very much, he had not acted in his son's best interest. He had not sent a clear message.

Let's rewrite the bike-parking script with love and learning as the themes. When Dad spotted the bike parked in a forbidden place, Dad might have called out to his son, "Come here, Son! Let's talk." Dad could kneel by his boy and ask, "Did you notice where you parked your bike?" It seems likely that the boy would immediately remember the rule. Dad could show compassion. "It's hard to remember when you're in a hurry. What could we do to help you remember?" The son might suggest, "Dad, could we take some chalk and draw a parking place for my bike on the floor?" Because the son was a vital part of the solution, he is much more likely to remember it.

With this approach, the parent sends a clear message: "I love you, Son. And I want to help you grow toward peaceful, loving, safe, adulthood."

Reflection

Think of a time when you have sent a clear message to one of your children when you were tempted to send a mixed or angry message. How did it feel? What helped you get there? How can you get there again? How can you make that experience more common for you?

Applying this Strategy

☐ I don't think this will work for me.
☐ This is something I am already good at and use regularly to good effect.
☐ This is something I haven't tried but would like to try.
Next time [insert your parenting dilemma] happens,

I'm going to try [insert your personal solution that
applies this strategy].

> Write a plan.
>
> Visualize yourself doing it.

☐ This is something I have tried but need to practice.

> Next time [insert your parenting dilemma] happens,
> I'm going to try [insert your personal solution that
> applies this strategy].
>
> Write a plan.
>
> Visualize yourself doing it.

Notes on progress: _____

_____

_____

_____

_____

50.

Get the Help of Ancestors

In every family history there is a wealth of goodness. Some of it may have taken colorful forms. Some of it may only be partially known. But we can all be enriched by knowing, loving, and selectively emulating our forebears.

When our children were small, we lived just around the corner from Nancy's grandparents. That meant that our children got to see their great-grandparents almost daily!

We used to go over to their house on Sunday afternoons and listen to their life stories. We also enjoyed their homespun poems and songs. Our children came to know them as friends. When we want to inspire them to greater ingenuity we remind them of Grandpa Les and the carts he made from castoff lawnmowers to help widow ladies haul things around their yards. When we want to encourage our children to kindness, we reminded them of Grandma Stella's loving, patient service. Their grandparents provide a real and inspiring energy for their own learning and growing.

Many of us have lost ancestors to death. Some we never knew. Some years ago I was studying my great-grandfather's life. The more I learned of him the more I wanted to become friends with this good man who died almost two decades before I was born. I yearned to sit and talk with him.

I wondered, "How can I visit with Grandpa Ben?" As I studied the matter, my path seemed clear. I could read his 1,054 page journal. I can read his letters and writings. I can study what he chose to do with his life. I have even read the books that were his favorites.

Then, when I have felt lonely or confused, I have sought counsel from my wise grandpa. I should promptly admit that I have never heard his voice audibly. But I have felt his encouragement and love in my life. I have been blessed by his example. And our children and grandchildren have been blessed by their ancestors as we tell them stories filled with adventure, goodness, struggle, and service.

Whatever the nature of our own family stories, there are priceless lessons to be learned from those who went before us. Our lives are enriched when we let our ancestors take part in them.

Reflection: Think of a ways you have been blessed by ancestors—or think of ways you could get their help. How did it—or could it—feel? What helped you get there? How can you get there again? How can you make that experience more common for you?

Applying this Strategy

☐ I don't think this will work for me.

☐ This is something I am already good at and use regularly to good effect.

☐ This is something I haven't tried but would like to try.

>   Next time [insert your parenting dilemma] happens, I'm going to try [insert your personal solution that applies this strategy].

>>   Write a plan.

>>   Visualize yourself doing it.

☐ This is something I have tried but need to practice.

>   Next time [insert your parenting dilemma] happens, I'm going to try [insert your personal solution that applies this strategy].

>>   Write a plan.

>>   Visualize yourself doing it.

Notes on progress: _____

_____

_____

_____

_____

_____

Conclusion

I hope this book has been useful to you. I hope it has given specific ideas and general encouragement. It may also have given some pain.

Yet I believe that pain is our friend. Just as the person with a numb foot runs the risk of injuring the foot unawares, so the person who is unaware of shortcomings runs the risk of harming his or her children unawares.

Mercifully, life discloses our shortcomings to us in manageable doses. As we discover them we can seek the solutions that will strengthen our parenting. Rather than do more of what does not work, we can seek new tools to add to our parenting toolbox. Our weaknesses become our strengths as they cause us to grow.

It is not the parent who seems to do it all perfectly who is to be admired. It is the one who recognizes his or her own failings and is willing to keep growing. Parenting classes may give us good ideas for dealing with children. Talking with wise and tender friends may help us. But if we are to excel at parenting, we must become the loving, good people we once dreamed of being. That doesn't happen overnight.

It should be no surprise that some of the greatest challenges of our lives come in parenting and family life. Only a task that demands the sacrifice of all our pride, all our self-importance, and all our stubbornness has the power to make us what we yearn to be.

Occasionally in our parenting journey we may be weary and downcast. We may be tempted to settle for mediocre parenting. But a better strategy is to rest as long as needed before seeking additional challenges.

Parenting is especially frustrating for those who have perfectionist tendencies. Parenting is a messy business. It can make us crazy. Or it can teach us to be patient with ourselves—to allow time to become the parents we yearn to be.

When I was a young father I often played a stalling game with my son Andy. He would often ask me to take a walk around the block with him. I would tell him that I would be glad to go—as soon as I finished reading the paper. Andy saw through my ruse. "That's what you always say, Dad."

I had been caught. So I jumped up and said, "Let's go." I dashed out the front door and headed around the block. As I rounded the first corner, Andy was still back in the front yard inspecting stones and bugs. I yelled, "Come on, Andy! We've got to get around the block!"

I wanted to be a good dad. I loved my son. But I was stingy with my time.

Often we turn children away as an interruption or an intrusion. They invite us to invest in that which is most durable and meaningful: humanness. It can be our goal to offer graciousness and love to our children. Generations will be blessed by our investment.

We become soft-spoken parents as we seek such humble things as a child's comfort and happiness. When Andy—or one of his children—wants to take a walk around the block, I hope I will always be available. I hope I will drop the paper and take his hand and let him lead me toward goodness.

None of this is easy. None of it is natural—since it is our natures to take care of ourselves. But it is possible.

Perhaps my all-time favorite parenting story is of a kindergartner named Terry who showed up at school one day with a note pinned to his jacket. He displayed the note proudly to his classmates.

Eventually the teacher spotted the note. Wondering if it had important instructions for her, she asked Terry, "Would you like me to read your note?" "Yes, I would," he replied.

The teacher removed the note and read, "Terry was unhappy this morning because his sister had a note and he did not. So this is Terry's note, and now he is happy."

That is goodness.

Notes

1. Haim G. Ginott, *Between Parent and Child* (New York: Three Rivers Press, 2003), xiii.

2. Frederick Buechner, *Wishful Thinking* (San Francisco: Harper & Row, 1993), 2.

3. http://www.quotationsbook.com/authors/4222/Byron_J._Langenfield/.

4. "Francis Bacon Quotes," http://www.brainyquote.com/quotes/quotes/f/francisbac133639.html.

5. E. Sigsgaard, *Scolding: Why It Hurts More Than It Helps* (New York: Teachers College Press, 2005), 143.

6. http://www.ushistory.org/paine/crisis/singlehtml.htm

7. A. Christensen and N. S. Jacobson, *Reconcilable Differences* (New York: Guilford, 2000), 17.

8. Frederick Buechner, *Wishful Thinking* (San Francisco: Harper & Row, 1993), 2.

9. Carol Tavris, *Anger: The Misunderstood Emotion* (New York: Simon and Schuster, 1983), 123.

10. Carol Tavris, *Anger: The Misunderstood Emotion* (New York: Simon and Schuster, 1983), 247.

11. Carol Tavris, *Anger: The Misunderstood Emotion* (New York: Simon and Schuster, 1983), 159.

12. Carol Tavris, *Anger: The Misunderstood Emotion* (New York: Simon and Schuster, 1983), 290.

13. Jonathan Haidt, *The Happiness Hypothesis* (New York: Basic Books, 2006), 73.

14. Jeffrey R. Holland, "Within the Clasp of Your Arms," *Ensign*, May 1983, 37.

15. Jonathan Haidt, *The Happiness Hypothesis* (New York: Basic Books, 2006), 78.

16. Ibid., xi.

17. Ibid., 80.

18. Mary Christensen, "BYU Today," *BYU Magazine*, December 1984, 4.

19. Jonathan Haidt, *The Happiness Hypothesis* (New York: Basic Books, 2006).

20. Ibid., 79.

21. S. T. Fiske and S. E. Taylor, *Social Cognition* (Reading, MA: Addison-Wesley, 1984), 88.

22. Jonathan Haidt, *The Happiness Hypothesis* (New York: Basic Books, 2006), 71.

23. Carol Lynn Pearson, "Secrets," *New Era*, March 1984, 17.

24. "Quotes by Bob Goddard," http://www.zaadz.com/quotes/Bob_Goddard/.

25. *Reader's Digest Pocket Treasury of Great Quotations* (Pleasantville, N.Y: Reader's Digest, 1975), xx.

26. Story adapted from H. W. Goddard's "Divine parenting: The atonement of Jesus Christ is the key," *My Soul Delighteth in the Scriptures: Personal and Family Applications*, eds. H. W. Goddard and R. H. Cracroft (Salt Lake City, UT: Bookcraft, 1999).

27. Haim G. Ginott, *Teacher and Child* (New York: MacMillan, 1972), 179.

28. See John M. Gottman, *Why Marriages Succeed or Fail* (New York: Simon and Schuster, 1994).

29. As quoted by Vaughn J. Featherstone in "The Torchbearer," *Speeches*, 5 June 1983, Brigham Young University, http://speeches.byu.edu/reader/reader.php?id=6871.

30. L. J. Peters, *Peter's Quotations: Ideas for Our Time* (New York: Bantam, 1977).

31. William Shakespeare, *Hamlet*, III, ii, 239.

32. Matthew 12:34, KJV.

33. See Martin E. P. Seligman, *Authentic Happiness* (New York: Free Press, 2002). This book is not only an excellent summary of the research on happiness, it is also one of the best psychology books written in decades.

34. Fred B. Bryant and Joseph Veroff, *Savoring: A New Model of Positive Experience.* (Mahwah, NJ: Erlbaum, 2007), 69.

35. See Martin Seligman's *Learned Optimism* (New York: Free Press, 1998).

36. Van Wyck Brooks, *A Chillmark Miscellany: Essays Old and New* (New York: Octagon Books, 1973).

37. *USA Today*, March 30, 1995

38. L. J. Peters, *Peter's Quotations: Ideas for Our Time* (New York: Bantam, 1977), 6.

39. Haim Ginott, *Between Parent and Child* (New York: Three Rivers Press, 2003), 47.

40. Gottman's best books include *The 7 Principles for Making Marriage Work* and *Why Marriages Succeed or Fail.*

41. See www.arfamilies.org for more information about these languages of love.

42. For recommended books on special issues, see *Authoritative Guide to Self-Help Resources in Mental Health* (New York: The Guilford Press, 2003).

43. See the full speech at http://speeches.byu.edu/reader/reader.php?id=848.

44. Quoted from A. Synnott, "Little angels, little devils: A sociology of children," *Canadian Review of Sociology and Anthropology*, 20(1), (1983), 79–95.

45. R. Byrne, *1911 Best Things Anybody Ever Said* (New York: Fawcett

Columbine, 1988), 194, and A.M. Nicholi, *The Question of God* (New York: Free Press, 2002), 181.

46. D. Beekman, *The Mechanical Baby* (Chicago: Chicago Review Press, 1977), 188.

47. J. Rosemond, *John Rosemond's Six-Point Plan for Raising Happy, Healthy Children* (New York: Andrews & McMeel, 1989), 190.

48. Quoted from D. Beekman, *The Mechanical Baby* (Chicago: Chicago Review Press, 1977), 20.

49. J. B. Watson, *Psychological Care of Infant and Child* (New York: W. W. Norton, 1928), 41.

50. Quoted from D. Beekman, *The Mechanical Baby* (Chicago: Chicago Review Press, 1977), 47.

51. Harry Emerson Fosdick, *The Meaning of Faith* (New York: Association Press, 1918), 89.

52. A. H. Maslow, *Motivation and Personality* (New York: Harper & Row 1954/1970), 118, 122.

53. See B. C. Rollins and D. L. Thomas, "Parental Support, Power, and Control Techniques in the Socialization of Children," *Contemporary Theories about The Family, Volume I.* ed. W. R. Burr, R. Hill, R. I. Nye, & I. L. Reiss (New York: Free Press, 1979), 317–364.

54. This story is adapted from *The Frightful and Joyous Journey of Family Life* by the author.

55. Matthew 5:44, KJV.

56. John Gottman, *Raising an Emotionally Intelligent Child* (New York: Simon and Schuster, 1998), 69–70.

57. Haim G. Ginott, *Between Parent and Child* (New York: Three Rivers Press, 2003), 117.

58. For more ideas on being strategic, see David Borgenicht and James Grace's *How to Con Your Kid* (Philadelphia: Quirk Books, 2005).

59. This story is adapted from *The Frightful and Joyous Journey of Family Life* by the author.

Index